America Divided

America Divided

Star Parker

Creators Publishing
Hermosa Beach, CA

Cover art by Kelly Evans

CREATORS PUBLISHING
737 3rd St
Hermosa Beach, CA 90254
310-337-7003

Although the author and publisher have made every effort to ensure that the information in this book was correct at press time, the author and publisher do not assume and hereby disclaim any liability to any party for any loss, damage or disruption caused by errors or omissions, whether such errors or omissions result from negligence, accident or any other cause.

ISBN (print): 978-1-949673-18-0
ISBN (ebook): 978-1-949673-17-3

First Edition
Printed in the United States of America
1   3   5   7   9   10   8   6   4   2

A Note From the Publisher

Since 1987, Creators has syndicated many of your favorite columns to newspapers. In this digital age, we are bringing collections of those columns to your fingertips. This will allow you to read and reread your favorite columnists, with your own personal digital archive of their work.

—Creators Publishing

Contents

Optimism About Trump in 2018	1
Trump Can Take Credit for Black Unemployment Drop	3
Republicans Must Lead Abortion Debate	6
Trump Acknowledges National School Choice Week	9
Bogus Racist Claims Agains Trump	12
Celebrate Black History by Promoting Ownership	15
A New Look Into Poverty in America	18
Investing In Opportunity	21
Frederick Douglass and Gun Control	24
What's Driving the Opioid Crisis?	27
What's Happening to Our Young Men?	30
GOP Narrative on PA-18 Is Wrong	33
Gun Control Movement Polar Opposite of Civil Rights Movement	36
Trump Should Focus on Debt Crisis Rather Than Trade	39
Trump's Vitally Important Anti-Poverty Initiative	42
Who Is Jim Jordan?	45
Michelle Wolf vs Mike Pence	47
Draining the Food Stamp Swamp	49
President Trump and the Israel Test	51
A First Step for Prison Reform	54
Stop Government-Supported Abortion, Family Planning	57
Will More Blacks Vote Republican?	60
Why Can't We Fix Social Security and Medicare?	63
Do Christians Have a Future in LGBTQ America?	66
America Divided Against Itself	69
The Demagoguery of Alexandria Ocasio-Ortiz	72
Abortion and the Constitution	75
Jim Jordan, Brett Kavanaugh and Journalism By Innuendo	78

Senate Should Pass the First Step   81
The Trump, GOP Economic Recovery   84
Lessons from Apple at a Trillion Dollars   87
Urban Violence Begins in Broken Homes   89
King's Dream Still Relevant Today   92
Republicans Can, Must Keep Control in Midterms   95
The Flawed Retrospectives on John McCain   98
School Disciplinary Policies Must Be Local   100
Feinstein v. Kavanaugh   103
Kavanaugh Show Will Help Republicans in November   106
Pro-Abortion Left vs. Kavanaugh   109
Will Kavanaugh Realign Racial Politics?   111
Midterms About Future of American Freedom   114
It's Democrats Who Shred American Values   117
Fake News Threatens Our National Health and Wealth   120
The Battle to MAGA Continues   123
Republican Opportunity With Young Blacks   126
A Lesson in Racial Politics from Florida   129
When Democrats Win, Freedom Loses   132
Thinking About What's Right in America   135
Family Breakdown Explains Social Unrest   137
Trump's Important New Africa Strategy   140
Protect Our Nation. Build the Wall   143
About the Author   146

Optimism About Trump in 2018

January 3, 2018

President Trump took office at the beginning of 2017 swimming in a sea of negativity.

Some predicted that he wouldn't make it through the year. Some predicted that he even if he did, he would fail to get any major legislation passed.

Pew Research Center reported that 62 percent of the news stories about Trump's first 60 days were negative, compared to 20 percent in President Obama's first 60 days and 28 percent in Bush's and Clinton's.

But those who voted for Trump wanted something completely different, and Trump is not disappointing them. As he moves forward in Washington with his own style of doing business, it brings to mind Frank Sinatra's classic song, "My Way."

Indeed, Trump is doing it his way. But what is causing doubters to sit up is that he is accomplishing in a big way.

The economy is growing like it hasn't in years, the most sweeping tax reform since 1986 has been passed, and he is deregulating. The number of pages in the Federal Register — where new regulations are published — is now two-thirds of where it stood in the Obama years.

Trump has already put his stamp on the nation, which will have repercussions for years, in his impressive conservative judicial appointments — 12 of his federal appeals court judge nominations have been confirmed by the Senate — and Neil Gorsuch has taken Antonin Scalia's seat on the Supreme Court.

With two Supreme Court justices over 80 — Anthony Kennedy and Ruth Bader Ginsburg — chances are that Trump will have an opportunity to place another solid conservative on the Supreme Court in the course of his first term.

Reports are that Trump will meet with Senate Majority leader McConnell and House Speaker Paul Ryan soon at Camp David to discuss legislative plans for 2018.

Major campaign issues still on the table are immigration reform, welfare reform and national infrastructure investments.

It is reasonable to expect that the product of these deliberations will reflect a combination of idealism — what they believe are national priorities — and political realism — what they see as doable in the existing political environment.

Certainly, McConnell's challenge in the Senate has increased with his Republican margin now a razor-thin 51 to 49.

On the other hand, in our unconventional president we have a man with plans to accomplish — his way.

Perhaps Trump fulfilled his campaign promise to recognize Jerusalem as the capital city of Israel to show that he is willing to do what he sees as the right thing despite great opposition.

In immigration reform and welfare reform, we have two issues vitally in need of attention, both with huge impacts on the nation and both very politically difficult.

But the inability of Washington to fix what is broken in our nation is what drove so many voters to Trump. If Trump ignores or forgets this, then it will turn him into just another politician. My guess is that this is an intolerable and indigestible fate to Donald Trump.

So I am optimistic that 2018 will bring more unexpected accomplishments from Trump, as he carries forward promises from his campaign.

That is, to turn the country back to its people, to re-unify the country under its founding ideals, and for all Americans to feel part of the American enterprise.

He said it memorably in his inaugural address. "And whether a child is born in the urban sprawl of Detroit, or the windswept plains of Nebraska, they look up at the same night sky, they fill their hearts with the same dreams, and they are infused with the breath of life by the same almighty creator."

I'm looking forward to a great 2018.

Trump Can Take Credit for Black Unemployment Drop

January 10, 2018

There's plenty to celebrate in the December Bureau of Labor Statistics report showing black unemployment at 6.8 percent, the lowest ever since they started reporting the data in 1972.

President Trump tweeted out his excitement and, of course, took credit for the good news. Has there ever been a politician who didn't take credit for good news on his watch (or rationalize away responsibility for bad news)?

The president's detractors, of course, wasted no time in challenging him, pointing out that unemployment rates have been dropping since the economic recovery started, well before Trump took office. Trump, they say, is as responsible for this latest monthly drop as he is for the morning sunrise.

It seems to me quite reasonable for Trump to take credit for this. There are, indeed, positive things happening as result of his leadership — deregulation, a new tax bill, overall business-friendly policies and rhetoric. These things create a business environment of optimism and confidence, which drives investment and increases demand for labor.

However, rather than obsessing about what particular politician to praise or excoriate for certain economic results, our discussion should be about policies and not about personalities. Let's savor this news but not lose our sobriety regarding the great task before us in this community.

The latest 6.8 percent black unemployment figure sounds great for blacks. But not for whites. The white rate for December was 3.7 percent. Why should there be celebrations that the black rate is "only" 3.1 percentage points higher than the white rate? Why should there be a different economic standard for blacks?

Black unemployment rates have averaged twice the white rate since 1972.

Black poverty rates are around twice the national average.

Black income and household wealth have hardly changed, remaining a fraction of that of whites.

This is the conversation we should be having. When do all American citizens participate equally in our national economic cornucopia?

Donald Trump was onto something when he asked blacks, during the presidential campaign, "What do you have to lose?"

Trump is offering a mindset that blacks should relish. A completely new and different reality. The cultural and political reality that blacks have turned to for years — big government — is the reason these gaps persist. It's time for something new.

Black unemployment peaked at 16.8 percent in March 2010 during President Obama's efforts to recover from the 2007-2008 economic collapse.

But the irony is that the collapse was driven by government policies put in place to help low-income Americans to make housing purchases. Contrary to what Barack Obama pitched to the country — blaming business and claiming the problem was insufficient government and regulation — American Enterprise Institute scholar Peter Wallison has shown the opposite.

Government policies mandating higher quotas of mortgages for low- to moderate-income borrowers put an increasing percentage of subprime mortgages on the market. By 2008, according to Wallison, 56 percent of the mortgages acquired by Fannie Mae and Freddie Mac — the two massive government-backed mortgage companies — were in this category.

Then everything collapsed.

An ocean of new regulations on financial services, enacted as part of the Dodd-Frank Act, was the Democratic Congress' answer to their own misdiagnosed analysis of what caused the collapse. As a result, we had a slower-than-normal economic recovery.

These are the discussions we need today. How do we get out of the big government mindset that has been a drag on our economy and has perpetuated economic underperformance in low-income communities?

In this context, Trump is right to boast. He is bringing badly needed new thinking on issues concerning low-income America. It's already making a difference.

Republicans Must Lead Abortion Debate

January 17, 2018

This year, as every year, I will be joining the hundreds of thousands who will be arriving in Washington, D.C., for the March for Life. March for Life notes the anniversary of the Roe v. Wade decision, Jan. 22, 1973, which legalized abortion on demand in our country.

The event has taken place every year since 1973 and will continue to take place every year until this disastrous and destructive decision is reversed.

Those who come to Washington express the breadth and depth of the resolve they hold for enshrining respect for the sanctity of life as part of our national culture.

They often brave the hostile elements of winter in our nation's capital. And have also braved many different political climates.

Fortunately, this year, the pro-life political climate has dramatically improved.

Operation Rescue, one the nation's leading activist pro-life Christian organizations, has named President Donald Trump its Pro-Life Person of the Year.

Last October, the House passed the Pain-Capable Unborn Child Protection Act. This legislation prohibits abortion after 20 weeks, the point at which it's estimated that the unborn child can feel pain.

Trump has indicated that he is ready to sign the bill into law. In order for this to happen, it must pass the Senate. However, there is considerable doubt that Majority Leader Mitch McConnell can muster the necessary 60 votes, particularly now that the Republican count in the Senate is down to 51.

Nevertheless, the push should be made in the Senate, and there are indications that the vote will take place.

Today's political landscape is characterized by increased partisan polarization, and abortion is no exception.

According to a 2017 Gallup poll, 71 percent of Democrats self-identify as "pro-choice" compared with 36 percent of Republicans — a difference of 35 percentage points. Sixteen years ago, in 2001, the gap between Democrats and Republicans on this issue was 26 points. The 71 percent "pro-choice" figure among Democrats in 2017 was the highest it's been in the last 17 years.

The nation's highest abortion rates are among black and Hispanics, both of whom vote disproportionately for Democrats. So, as in other areas, these minority communities are not getting the leadership they need in the Democratic politicians they vote for.

It's why Republicans should push for floor votes on abortion. It provides an opportunity to push Democrats and raise awareness among their constituents about this issue.

Black women constitute 6 percent of our population, yet they account for 35 percent of abortions. How can Democrats possibly be serving this community by supporting and encouraging this disaster?

It's vital for blacks, and for all Americans, to understand that abortion is not an issue that can be viewed in isolation. Lack of respect for the sanctity of life spills over into other critical areas of human behavior.

Thus it is no accident that the years since the Roe v. Wade decision have been years in which the American family has collapsed.

In 1960, 73 percent of all children were living with two parents in a first marriage. By 2014, this was down to 46 percent.

In 2014, 54 percent of black children were living with a single parent. Seventy-one percent of black babies were born to unwed mothers in 2014 compared with 40 percent in 1960.

Research is overwhelming regarding the centrality of a healthy family structure to success in life. There is little question that the deep issues in black communities today tie to family collapse.

And at the core of that collapse is the absence of reverence for the sanctity of life.

There is no issue more central to our national moral, physical and fiscal health than abortion. And the partisan implications are clear.

Republicans must help lead blacks and Hispanics out of the darkness in which the Democratic Party is holding them hostage.

Trump Acknowledges National School Choice Week

January 24, 2018

Amidst the ongoing political noise and distractions in Washington, D.C., President Trump continues to focus on and address the nation's most deep-seated problems.

In the wake of signing a temporary funding bill to get the government back open, the president directed attention to one of our biggest problems. Education.

Trump proclaimed the week of Jan. 22 as National School Choice Week. National School Choice Week began in 2011. Trump's proclamation notes a commitment to "a future of unprecedented educational achievement and freedom of choice."

We have a president keenly aware of the need to fundamentally change the status quo in our education system. And one indication of this pledge is his selection of Betsy DeVos as secretary of education.

DeVos spoke recently at the American Enterprise Institute in Washington, and she delivered remarks about the state of education in America that were courageous.

She spoke about the mediocre performance of our students, compared to those in other nations of the world, in the Program for International Student Assessment. Why, when we have among the highest education spending in the world per student, should American students be ranking 23 in reading, 25 in science and 40 in math?

Even by our own measures in our National Assessment of Educational Progress, known as the Nation's Report Card, the results remain disappointing.

In the case of our black children, the results are dismal. In the 2015 NAEP math scores, 17 percent of black fourth-graders and 11 percent of black eighth-graders performed at "proficient" levels. In reading, 16 percent of black fourth-graders and 15 percent of black eighth-graders were "proficient."

Billions have been spent on education with little to show for the efforts.

DeVos' bold bottom line:

"Federally mandated assessments. Federal money. Federal standards. All originated in Washington, and none solved the problem."

We had the No Child Left Behind Act under President Bush, and the Race to the Top Fund under President Obama. Different approaches, but the same power, control and money coming from Washington.

"The bottom line is simple," said DeVos. "Federal education reforms have not worked as hoped."

A number of left-wing journalists today are questioning the mental health of our president.

But DeVos' brutally honest assessment about the state of education in our country shows that if we have a mental health problem, it resides with those who keep pushing more and more government when this approach consistently fails us.

"Insanity," reportedly said Einstein, "is doing the same thing over and over again and expecting different results."

How, in a country so diverse in values as ours, can we possibly have government controlling how *all* children are educated?

How, in a country that values human freedom, as we allegedly do, can we prevent parents from deciding how to educate their children?

Today, there are 63 different school choice programs across the nation involving 469,000 individuals, according to EdChoice. But total expenditures on school choice programs are still less the 0.4 percent of the $586.8 billion we spend annually on K-12 education.

One bombshell that Betsy DeVos dropped in her AEI remarks is that federally imposed performance standards in reading and math — know as Common Core — is "dead" at the Department of

Education. Not because of ideology. Because these federal standards demonstrably do not work.

Few would disagree that America's economic and political freedom is the source of our strength and prosperity. Yet, how can we deny America's secret of success to the marketplace of greatest importance to our future — education?

It's not unreasonable to think that one reason the stock market is booming is that our American leadership has the courage to bring real change. Educational freedom is at the core of a new American prosperity.

Bogus Racist Claims Against Trump

January 31, 2019

As President Trump lays out and implements his vision for American success — via his campaign slogan, "Make America Great Again" — there remain defiant naysayers.

Among the most defiant are those who want to talk about race.

They oppose Trump, claiming he is biased against minorities. Unfortunately, talking about race is a great diversion from the discussion about the ideas and policies we need as a nation to move forward.

The proposition that America is a country defined by a set of founding principles that are true for all is itself taken as racism. It flies in the face of the identity politics, so loved by the left, that sees American greatness not in universal principles but in giving credence to the claims of interest groups and responding to these claims through new laws and court decisions.

African-Americans are, of course, the poster children of interest groups, because of the history of injustices to which blacks can point.

But we seem to forget that in order for there to be sense of injustice and wrong, we need principles defining what is just and right.

If we look back to Barack Obama's famous speech at the 2004 Democratic Convention — the speech that put him on the political map — he sounds like Donald Trump.

"Now even as we speak," he said, "there are those preparing to divide us, the spin masters, and negative ad peddlers, who embrace the politics of anything goes.

"Well I say to them tonight, there is not a liberal America or a conservative America; there's the United States of America.

"There's not a black America and a white America and Latino America and Asian America; there's the United States of America. "We are one people, all of us pledging allegiance to the Stars and Stripes, all of us defending the United States of America."

When Trump makes these same points, because he is de facto delegitimizing interest group politics, many blacks — and, of course, most liberals — call him racist.

Granted, our president is not always careful with his rhetoric. But policy and principles are what we should be looking at, not rhetoric.

We might recall that four years after Obama stated those inspiring words, he was quoted during the 2008 campaign, speaking about working-class Americans hard hit by the recession, saying, "They get bitter, they cling to guns or religion, or antipathy to people who aren't like them, or anti-immigrant sentiment, or anti-trade sentiment as a way to explain their frustrations."

The point is that the difference between Obama and Trump is not prejudice toward white working-class Americans versus prejudice toward minorities.

The difference is in their ideas of what makes America great. One sees big, activist government as what defines us. The other sees limited government and individual freedom as what defines us.

Trump is bringing back individual freedom and economic freedom. And it's working. Deregulation and a new tax-cutting law are freeing up the marketplace, and the economy is seriously picking up steam.

The latest Wells Fargo/Gallup Small Business Index, which measures "small-business owners' attitudes about a wide-variety of factors affecting their businesses," shows the highest score in 11 years.

Fifty-two percent of "business owners reported their revenue increased a little or a lot over the past 12 months ... the highest reading on this measure since 2007."

Is this good for blacks? A growing, churning economy is good for *every* American.

Economic growth is the engine of opportunity.

Let's not get diverted by racial rhetoric. Individual freedom, not interest group politics, is the platform through which every American, of every background, can realize their potential and participate in a growing, job-creating economy.

Celebrate Black History by Promoting Black Ownership

February 7, 2018

I have long been in favor of reforming Social Security by changing it to a system of personally owned retirement accounts.

Instead of paying a payroll tax, with the U.S. government telling you what you'll get when you retire, you take ownership of that money — the payroll tax — and invest in your own retirement account.

I am for IRAs not the IRS.

This is a good time to bring this up, following a big drop in the stock market. Such a drop, to many, is exactly the reason to not do this reform.

As of this writing, the stock market dropped around 5 percent. What is officially called a market "correction" is a drop of 10 percent.

However, over the last year, the stock market has increased 26 percent. Since the presidential election in November 2016, it's up 35 to 40 percent.

The point is, stocks are a long-term proposition and so is retirement investing. Although gyrations are part of the day-to-day reality of stocks, over the long haul they provide positive returns. Because they reflect the underlying health of the economy, if stocks aren't healthy in the long run, it means the country is not healthy in the long run. The historical annual average return on stocks is 8 percent.

Stocks are like life. Time, optimism and faith smooth out the ups and downs. I'll take the ups and downs of a free life and a free marketplace over turning control of my life over to politicians.

In 2010, William Shipman and Peter Ferrara published an analysis in The Wall Street Journal of what would have happened to a couple who invested their payroll tax in their own retirement account, over 44 years, and then retired in 2009, the year after the huge stock market drop in 2008. In 2008, their account lost 37 percent of its value.

Even this huge one-year drop did not offset the accumulated positive gains. The average return from 1965 to 2009 was 6.75 percent and "would still pay them about 75 percent more than Social Security would have."

But even this is not the main point. Although it makes sense to be invested in stocks over a 40-year plus working life, no one is saying you have to do it. You can buy bonds or put the money in a bank CD.

The main point is that every citizen should be free to have these options.

There are particularly important implications here to black Americans.

Per the Federal Reserve, in 2016 median black family net worth was $17,600, about 10 percent of median white family net worth.

Thirty-four percent of black families have retirement accounts, compared with 60 percent of white families, and 31 percent of blacks have some kind of stock ownership compared with 61 percent of whites. And only 8 percent of blacks have received wealth through inheritance compared with 26 percent of whites.

Social Security provides survivor benefits to spouses and unmarried minor children. As of 2012, 36 percent of blacks over 25, compared with 16 percent of whites, had never been married. Because of the sorry state of marriage and family in black America, a large percentage of black Americans will have paid into Social Security over a full working life, and those benefits will just go up in smoke when they pass away.

With all the handwringing about gaps in wealth and income in our country, if we were serious we would have policies that promote, rather than prohibit, ownership.

Let's at least give low-income Americans the option to get out of Social Security and invest in personal retirement accounts to build ownership and wealth that can be bequeathed to others.

This would be a great way to celebrate Black History Month.

A New Look Into Poverty in America

February 14, 2018

In 2015, as told on the Center for Advancing Opportunity website, Johnny C. Taylor Jr., then-president of the Thurgood Marshall College Fund, heard libertarian billionaire businessman Charles Koch, in a TV interview, discussing eliminating barriers to opportunity.

Taylor reached out to Koch, and the result was a Koch contribution of $25.6 million to the TMCF to establish the Center for Advancing Opportunity.

Although there is no shortage of research on the causes and challenges of poverty in America, CAO's innovation is to study the problem by going into these communities, seeing how the locals think and devising local solutions. The Center, according to Koch, "brings together students and faculty from Historically Black Colleges and Universities with community members to study and collect data about criminal justice, education, and entrepreneurship and formulate locally informed solutions to them."

Now CAO has brought in another partner, Gallup, and has released its first major survey: "The State of Opportunity in America: Understanding Barriers & Identifying Solutions."

The research examines "fragile" communities, defined as "areas with high proportions of residents who struggle financially in their daily lives and have limited opportunities for social mobility."

Gallup combined in-depth surveys of four such fragile communities — Birmingham, Alabama; Cleveland, Ohio; Fresno, California; Chicago, Illinois — with a national survey.

Sixty-six percent of these communities are black or Hispanic, 58 percent earn less than $34,999, and 12 percent of the population have a bachelor's degree or more.

The survey results point to some conclusions that are not so surprising, but also to some that are.

Not so surprising is that individuals in these communities are struggling. Forty-four percent say that there were times during the past year that they were unable to afford food. Forty percent say that they are "finding it difficult" or "very difficult" to get by on their current income.

Thirty-eight percent work full time for an employer. Fifty-one percent believe crime in their community has increased "over the last few years."

Only 32 percent strongly agree or agree that all children in their community have access to high-quality public schools.

But despite challenging life circumstances, individuals in these communities remain resilient and optimistic. This is the best and most encouraging news.

Sixty-eight percent of the residents of these communities, compared to 79 percent of all Americans, agree that Americans "can get ahead" by "working hard." Only 32 percent are pessimistic that everyone can "get ahead."

Twenty-one percent indicate plans to move in next 12 months. Fifty-nine percent say they would like to move. Changing a residence requires optimism and initiative. These are healthy signs of vitality in these distressed communities.

What concerns me are the perceptions that residents of these fragile communities have regarding policies that they say they think will improve their situations. Raise the minimum wage, more funds to public schools, more government spending.

This demonstrates the great need for conservative thought leaders to spend quality time in these communities educating residents about ideas that have failed — in fact, the very ideas residents think work — and discussing innovative ideas that can bring the results they seek.

How can we change the tax and regulatory realities of these communities to attract business? How can school vouchers and tax credits create schools that can serve the special needs of these communities? How can housing vouchers provide the flexibility for these individuals to benefit from government housing assistance but still allow them to move and choose where they want to live?

The partnership between Koch and the Thurgood Marshall College Fund is an exciting and innovative development. The meeting of minds between the libertarian Kochs and the largely traditionally Democratic communities of the Historically Black Colleges and Universities can produce new understanding and insights to fight the challenge of poverty in our country.

Investing in Opportunity

February 21, 2018

Included as part of the Tax Cuts and Jobs Act, signed into law by President Trump in December, was an important new initiative called the Investing in Opportunity Act.

The IIOA was a bipartisan initiative, sponsored by Republican Tim Scott and Democrat Cory Booker in the Senate, and Republican Pat Tiberi and Democrat Ron Kind in the House. It provides a major new platform for directing capital for business development into America's poorest communities.

This alone refutes claims from the political left that this tax bill was just for the wealthy.

The concept was started in 2015 with the appearance of the Economic Innovation Group in Washington, D.C. It's a new initiative of a group of high-tech entrepreneurs — leaders from companies like Facebook and Napster — to do nonpartisan work developing ideas to restore a dynamic American economy and bring vitality to the many parts of the country that are falling behind.

The first major paper produced was co-authored by two economists — Jared Bernstein, a Democrat, and Kevin Hassett, then of the American Enterprise Institute and now chairman of President Trump's Council of Economic Advisors.

The paper, titled "Unlocking Private Capital to Facilitate Economic Growth in Distressed Areas," laid the groundwork for the Investing in Opportunity Act.

Bernstein and Hassett wove together several key points.

First, large parts of the country — the most distressed communities — are not participating in the economic recovery.

Poverty rates, unemployment, income levels in these communities are far out of line with national averages.

The Economic Innovation Group has surveyed 26,000 ZIP codes nationwide, rating them according their state of economic well-being, and has published a Distressed Community Index. The conclusion — 52.3 million Americans, 1 in 6, live in economically distressed communities.

Second, Bernstein and Hassett surveyed the various programs over the years designed to bolster business investment in these communities and discussed why these programs have been disappointing.

And third, they pointed out what appears to be an exciting opportunity. With the stock market surging since the beginning of the economic recovery in 2009, investors are holding around $2.3 trillion in unrealized capital gains. Often, appreciated securities are not sold because of the capital gains taxes due when the sale is made.

Bernstein and Hassett's idea, which is now part of the IIOA, is to allow investors to defer and receive reductions in the tax liabilities on this $2.3 trillion if the funds are invested in Opportunity Zones — census tracts containing these most distressed communities.

Governors have until March 22 to designate up to 25 percent of the most economically distressed census tracts in their state as Opportunity Zones. Opportunity Zone Funds will be established as the entities through which the investments are made in these distressed communities.

Final details of the IIOA will be worked out as the Treasury Department writes the rules defining how it all will work. But those whose lives are rooted in these distressed communities should see this as an exciting opportunity and get involved to make the most of it.

Many churches operate nonprofit community development corporations whose purpose is developing businesses. Those operating these CDCs should be on top of emerging details of this program to see how they can attract investors into their communities.

Furthermore, appreciated capital is not limited to the stock market. It's also in real estate. Specifically, community leaders should apply pressure on absentee landlords whose abandoned properties in these communities are places of blight and crime. This could be a golden opportunity for these properties to be sold and the capital now tied up in blight can be redirected to productive economic development.

Kudos to the Economic Innovation Group for pioneering this idea and to Senators Scott and Booker and Congressmen Tiberi and Kind for getting it in the tax bill.

Frederick Douglass and Gun Control

February 28, 2018

President Trump has signed into law bipartisan legislation establishing the Frederick Douglass Bicentennial Commission to celebrate Douglass' life and work. I have been honored to be appointed, along with Dr. Alveda King, niece of Dr. Martin Luther King Jr., and others, to this commission.

Born into slavery 200 years ago, Douglass taught himself to read and write, escaped to freedom and became an anti-slavery and human rights activist, newspaper publisher and advisor to presidents.

I consider Douglass' life and struggles as I watch this latest round of public debate about the right of American citizens to bear arms. I watch with amazement the ease with which so many are ready to compromise the core freedoms that define us as Americans, for which so many have struggled and died.

In May of 1865, one month after the end of the Civil War, Douglass spoke to the American Anti-Slavery Society, convened at New York City's Church of the Puritans.

The topic of discussion was whether the society should continue its work in light of the formal abolition of slavery. By the end of that year, the 13th Amendment, prohibiting slavery in the United States, would be ratified.

Douglass's address was entitled "In What New Skin Will the Old Snake Come Forth?"

He spoke prophetically, questioning the value of the anti-slavery amendment if black Americans still would not be protected by rights guaranteed in the U.S. Constitution.

"...while the Legislatures of the South can take from him (the black man) the right to keep and bear arms, as they can ... the work of the Abolitionists is not finished."

Fast-forward 145 years to another black man, Otis McDonald, suing the city of Chicago because of its ordinance prohibiting him from owning a handgun to protect himself and his property from the vandalism and break-ins that were regularly taking place in his neighborhood.

McDonald's lawsuit made it to the Supreme Court, which ruled, in 2010, that states and localities cannot infringe on the Second Amendment protection for individuals to keep and bear arms.

This decision stemmed from the 14th Amendment, the second of the post-Civil War amendments to the Constitution. Whereas the 13th Amendment abolished slavery, the 14th Amendment guaranteed protection of constitutional rights in the states:

"No State shall make or enforce any law which shall abridge the privileges or immunities of citizens of the United States; nor shall any State deprive any person of life, liberty, or property without due process of the law."

This amendment addressed the concerns of Frederick Douglass that although slavery may have been abolished, states still had great latitude to deny citizens constitutional rights.

The Supreme Court decision of McDonald v. Chicago argued that the 14th Amendment "due process" clause protects citizens' Second Amendment right to keep and bear arms in the states.

Associate Justice Clarence Thomas, while supporting the majority decision, wrote a separate concurring opinion arguing that the 14th Amendment protection stems from the "privileges or immunities" clause.

"Privileges or immunities," argued Thomas, are our most fundamental rights as citizens. And this is what the right of American citizens to keep and bear arms is about.

Thomas, in his opinion, documents the bloody history of murder and lynching against blacks and white civil rights activists.

"Without federal enforcement of the inalienable right to keep and bear arms, these militias and mobs were tragically successful against the very people the 14th Amendment had just made citizens."

Freedom is not free, nor is it easy. The alternative to freedom is tyranny. Those who think it's a good idea to compromise our freedom rather than deal with its great challenges err tragically.

Frederick Douglass would surely be an NRA advocate today, and would be fighting to preserve our right to protect ourselves.

What's Driving the Opioid Crisis?

March 7, 2018

By now, most have heard about the deadly opioid epidemic that has struck our nation.

According to data compiled in a Kaiser Family Foundation report, there were 42,249 casualties in 2016 related to opioids. This is double the 21,089 reported in 2010.

For a little perspective, given all the attention guns are getting these days, per the FBI, in 2015 there were 13,455 murders, 9,616 committed with firearms.

What is driving this opioid crisis?

According to a recent report about opioids by the Social Capital Project, organized in the U.S. Senate, "the oversupply and abuse of legal prescription pain relievers is at the heart of the crisis."

This has led to action in Washington with legislation such as the Opioid Addiction Prevention Act, which would impose limits on opioid painkiller prescriptions.

However, Dr. Sally Satel, a psychiatrist and lecturer at Yale University School of Medicine and resident scholar at the American Enterprise Institute in Washington, D.C., challenges this picture, which she calls "a false narrative."

According to Satel, data show "that only a minority of people who are prescribed opioids for pain become addicted to them, and those who do become addicted and who die from painkiller overdoses tend to obtain these medications from sources other than their own physicians. Within the past several years, overdose deaths are overwhelmingly attributable not to prescription opioids but to illicit fentanyl and heroin. These 'street opioids' have become the engine of the opioid crisis in its current, and most lethal form."

Satel acknowledges the problem of overprescribed opioid painkillers being diverted to people other than the intended patient, but she doesn't see this as the core of today's crisis.

Furthermore, we don't want to get into a situation where doctors are intimidated from prescribing, or prevented from prescribing, painkillers that are justifiably needed.

I believe Satel zeroes in on the real heart of the crisis when she says, "What we need is demand-side policy. Interventions that seek to reduce the desire to use drugs, be they painkillers, or illicit opioids."

Here, I see an interesting parallel to the gun debate.

That is, the center of the deadly problem is with the disturbed user or perpetrator, rather than with the instrument — whether it is a gun or a drug. The instrument is the result rather than the cause.

The first impulse, particularly in a highly materialistic and secular culture like ours, is to see the problem in the thing rather than the person, because that's the easiest approach.

Looking at the demographics of the opioid crisis, a number of flashing lights emerge.

First, the perpetrators are disproportionately men (another parallel with the gun issue). Of the 42,249 opioid related deaths in 2016, 67 percent were men.

Also, as reported by the Social Capital Project, opioid casualties are disproportionately not married. In 2015, "never married and divorced individuals made up about 32 percent of the population but accounted for 71 percent of all opioid overdose deaths."

And opioid casualties appear disproportionately among the least educated. In 2015, "40 percent had no more than a high school diploma or equivalent, but they accounted for 68 percent of all opioid overdose deaths."

As policy makers in Washington and in state and local governments attempt to address this opioid crisis, looking to the usual policy tools like government programs and government spending, I think it's worth considering that what we're seeing may reflect a spiritual, cultural crisis.

There's a price to be paid when a society forsakes the spiritual for the purely material and when traditional institutions such as marriage and family are abandoned. It could be that as family and marriage break down, the first victims of this abandonment of spirit and tradition are our young men.

What's Happening to Our Young Men?

March 14, 2018

Writing last week about the opioid crisis, I suggested that, as we consider policy options for dealing with the problem, we consider that at least some part of it may reflect a spiritual, moral crisis in the country.

I noted that casualties from opioids show that they are disproportionately men, disproportionately divorced or never married, and disproportionately individuals with no more than a high school education.

We can look beyond the opioid crisis and see a broad, disturbing picture pointing to a social and spiritual crisis among our young men.

In 2016, Nicholas Eberstadt, a scholar at the American Enterprise Institute in Washington, D.C., published a book called "America's Invisible Crisis: Men Without Work."

He discusses what he calls a "flight from work" in which droves of our male population have disappeared from the work force.

The Bureau of Labor Statistics just issued its new jobs report, and the results were heartening. Data shows a return to growth in jobs in the American economy and return to the work force of many who dropped out during the years following the recent recession.

The labor force participation rate of prime-age working men ages 25-54, that is, the percentage working or actively seeking work, was 89.3 percent in February 2018.

Given that this rate was down to 88.4 late in 2011, we see progress here — good news.

However, Eberstadt points out that average labor force participation rate of these prime-age working men in 1965 was 96.6 percent.

"Expressed another way," says Eberstadt, "the proportion of economically inactive American men of prime working age leapt from 3.4 percent in 1965 to 11.8 percent in 2015, and remains at 11.5 percent today."

By my own calculations, almost 5 million prime-age working men have disappeared from the work force.

The U.S. population of men 25-54 today is 64.5 million. If their work force participation today was 96.6 percent, as it was in 1965, 62.3 million would be working or actively seeking work. But today's reported rate of 89.3 percent indicates that there are now 57.6 million prime-age men working or actively looking for work — 4.7 million less than there would have been at the 1965 rate.

How are these millions of men who have dropped out of the work force sustaining themselves?

According to Eberstadt, they get help from friends, family, and, of course, government.

Using Census Bureau data, Eberstadt reports "as of 2013, over three-fifths of prime-age men not in the labor force lived in homes that relied on at least one means-tested program for income. Some 41 percent of these men lived on food stamps, while just over half reported using Medicaid, a noncash benefit program."

Additional Census Bureau data, according to Eberstadt, shows that "in 2013, some 57 percent of prime-age unworking men were getting benefits from at least one government-disability program."

What is the profile of these prime-age unworking men?

They most likely have no more than a high school diploma, are not married, have no children or are not living with children they may have, are born in the USA and are black.

Although overall the workforce participation rate for black men is lower than that of white men, the cultural dynamics at play are more fundamental driving factors of what's going on than race.

For instance, Eberstatdt points out that "labor-force participation rates for white men today are lower than they were for black men in 1965."

Also, the labor-force participation rates for never-married white men are consistently lower, by about 3 percentage points, than for married black men.

We are paying a large social price for the widespread collapse of Christian values — in particular, the values of marriage and family. And our young men may be disproportionately bearing the brunt of this.

GOP Narrative on PA-18 Is Wrong

March 21, 2018

I'm perplexed why many in Republican circles are rationalizing and dismissing the gravity of the Democratic victory in the recent special election in Pennsylvania's 18th district.

My sentiments are more with Newt Gingrich, who is cautioning Republicans to view this as a wake-up call to a possible disaster in the fall elections in which the Congress could flip to Democrat control.

Pennsylvania's 18th congressional district is a poster child of Trump voters. As widely noted, Trump won this district by 20 points in 2016.

The district's electorate is 94 percent white, compared with 70 percent nationwide. In 2016, Trump won the white vote 58 percent to 37 percent. These are white working-class voters, exactly the voters who played a central role in flipping a number of blue states into the red column in 2016 and delivering the White House to Donald Trump.

So what happened in this election?

Some have suggested that Conor Lamb, the Democrat victor, essentially ran as a conservative and a Republican, and this explains his success.

If this is the case, then I've got some work to do to re-think my sense of what it means to be a conservative and a Republican.

Lamb was out front criticizing the tax cut bill just passed in the Republican congress, without a single Democratic vote, and signed into law by Trump.

According to Lamb, the tax bill was a "giveaway," most of which just went to and benefitted the "1 percent" — the wealthiest families in America.

Perhaps our new young congressman missed the news in the Bureau of Labor Statistics February jobs report reporting the addition of 313,000 new jobs — far above the average monthly jobs gain during this recent economic recovery. And more than 800,000 Americans joined the work force, which, according to The Wall Street Journal, was "the largest one-month labor-pool increase since 1983."

I can assure Conor Lamb that these hundreds of thousands going back to work as result of a freer economy and easing of a punishing tax code are not in the wealthiest 1 percent.

Lamb devoted a full campaign ad to attacking Paul Ryan's work to generate ideas to reform Social Security and Medicare.

Lamb said that working Americans "expect us to keep our promises to them."

This is liberal boilerplate, not Republican talking points.

We are already breaking our promises to working Americans. Social Security and Medicare Trustees report unfunded liabilities of Social Security and Medicare at more than $60 trillion, more than triple our GDP. These are benefits promised to Social Security and Medicare recipients for which there is no money. The system is broken and Paul Ryan is trying to find ways to fix it.

It shows Lamb's political skills that somehow he managed to create the impression that he is pro-life. Saying you are personally opposed to abortion but stating zero intention to work to change the current abortion laws in American, which is Lamb's position, translates into being pro-abortion.

Two of Newt's recommendations for addressing this looming electoral challenge facing Republicans are particularly worthy of attention.

First, start an intense national awareness building campaign about Republican and conservative values, with clarity about how they will help every American. Everyone should understand the moral and fiscal bankruptcy to which the liberal secular state is taking us and how God-given truths and freedom, which defined our founding, made American great and are vital for keeping it great.

Second, Republicans must expand the party base. Gingrich rightly points out the critical importance that Republicans build support among minorities.

There is great potential here. In 2016, 1.3 million blacks, 8 percent, voted for President Trump. However, according to Pew Research, although 10 percent of black Christian Protestants self-identify as Republicans, 36 percent identify as politically conservative. This spells opportunity — if the work is done.

Gun Control Movement Polar Opposite of Civil Rights Movement

March 28, 2018

Covering the pro-gun control March for Our Lives in Washington, CNN ran a headline that read, "They're marching through the same streets as Martin Luther King Jr. did — hoping for similar change."

The article then quoted a 16-year-old as saying, "The civil rights movement was started by teenagers."

How can we expect to properly deal with an issue as serious as guns and the Second Amendment when the media peddle such ignorance?

It should be sufficient to point out that Dr. King and Rosa Parks were not teenage activists.

But more seriously, it is critical to understand that this current movement to limit the ability of Americans to exercise their Second Amendment right to own a firearm is at total philosophical odds with what the civil rights movement aimed to accomplish.

The civil rights movement was about fixing what was broken in America regarding the ideals of individual freedom and dignity.

When King spoke his famous words at the National Mall in August 1963, his appeal was to perfect the American ideal. He called the "magnificent words of the Constitution and the Declaration of Independence" a "promissory note to which every American was to fall heir. This note was a promise that all men ... would be guaranteed the unalienable rights of life, liberty and the pursuit of happiness."

King's movement shone light on the fact that there was pain and suffering in the country because there were still Americans who were not free. That is what needed to be fixed.

Today's movement against guns and the Second Amendment aims in the opposite direction. The claim of this movement is that we have pain and suffering in our nation because we are too free. The marchers and others are telling us we can make a better nation by using the force of government to scale back our freedoms.

In a USA Today column, Obama-era Secretary of Education Arne Duncan and Dale Erquiaga, a former superintendent of public instruction for Nevada's schools, tell us: "Children should not have to pass through metal detectors to go to school. Nor should teachers have to arm themselves to keep students safe."

Why not?

Is having children walk through metal detectors to go to school too high a price to pay to avoid scaling back our constitutionally guaranteed freedoms? Is having armed guards and/or armed teachers too high a price to deal with the costs and demands of our free society, as opposed to dealing with these challenges by choosing to use government force to scale back our freedoms?

Perhaps metal detectors and other measures to make schools more secure and less vulnerable to attack would play an important role in our educational process to help our young people understand that freedom is not free.

We have a young generation in our country today from whom we ask nothing for the privilege of living in freedom. The idea that part of living free is taking personal responsibility has become a concept alien to many of our young Americans.

We might recall the fall of 1957, when President Dwight Eisenhower federalized the Arkansas National Guard, which Arkansas Gov. Orval Faubus had used to block nine black children from entering Little Rock's Central High School to attend school. Eisenhower then sent in more federal troops to protect these black children and their right to attend this school.

Eisenhower, who had served as supreme commander of Allied troops in Europe during World War II, understood force and understood freedom. He said it would be "a sad day for this country

... if schoolchildren can safely attend their classes only under the protection of armed guards."

The nation watched aghast as federal paratroopers were deployed to Central High School. It was an excruciatingly difficult decision for Eisenhower, but in the end, he concluded that he had to do it "to preserve the institutions of free government."

Republicans might note Eisenhower's example and recall that in 1956, Republican Eisenhower received 39 percent of the black vote.

Trump Should Focus on Debt Crisis Rather Than Trade

April 10, 2018

Donald Trump achieved the presidency telling the American people he would "Make America Great Again."

Given that during eight years of Barack Obama's presidency there was not a single year in which national satisfaction, as measured by Gallup, averaged above 30 percent, tapping into Americans' general dissatisfaction with the state of the nation was good campaign strategy.

This February, national satisfaction reached the highest its been under Trump, 36 percent. However, in March it plunged back down to 28 percent. And this big drop was fueled by a big drop among Republicans. National satisfaction among Republicans dropped from 67 percent in February to 52 percent in March.

Maybe there's reason to believe that Trump's own Republican constituency is not buying that tariff saber-rattling and trade protectionism is what is going to make America "great again."

The stock market surged some 30 percent from Trump's election until the beginning of 2018. However, since the beginning of this year, with all the trade war rhetoric, it's now down 8 percent.

Estimated overall value of the U.S. stock market early 2018 was around $30 trillion. So 8 percent deterioration means a loss of wealth of $2.4 trillion.

A price tag of $2.4 trillion in lost wealth to allegedly combat a $376 billion trade deficit with China with tariffs suggests that this might not be the best course of action.

The trade deficit is the supposed boogeyman. In 2017, we sold $130 billion in product to China and bought $506 billion from them

— a $376 billion trade deficit. Suppose China just decided to stop selling to us and just bought from us? We'd have a $130 billion surplus with them. Would that be good?

Americans are buying $506 billion in raw materials and consumer goods from China because we want this stuff. It makes us better off. We like the low-priced products from China we find in our department stores. And the raw materials we buy from them result in cheaper finished products that we manufacture here in the U.S.

According to economics blogger Mark Perry, "38 Americans work in industries using steel and aluminum for every worker making steel or aluminum."

Veronique de Rugy of George Mason University's Mercatus Center reports that when George W. Bush imposed tariffs on steel in 2002, 200,000 workers in industries using steel lost their jobs the following year — more than the total number of jobs in the steel industry that year.

What was the 30 percent stock market gain from Trump's election until early 2018 telling us? I believe these gains reflected the deregulation over this period, capped off with passage of the tax bill in December 2017.

These are the kind of measures that "Make America Great Again." Measures that advance our economic freedom and move control of politicians and government out of our lives.

We lose when politicians start picking winners and losers, whether domestically or internationally. Let the marketplace pick winners and losers.

Where should we be directing our priorities now?

A group of Hoover Institution economists, including former Secretary of State George Shultz, just published an op-ed in The Washington Post about the dire implications of the looming debt crisis in our country.

They write that soon the national debt will reach $20 trillion — equal to the size of our entire GDP. This poses a serious threat to our economic well-being.

New projections from the Congressional Budget Office forecast unprecedented trillion dollar federal budget deficits as far as the eye can see.

Unrestrained spending produces these huge deficits, which we finance with debt. The main culprit, according to the Hoover experts, is entitlement programs — Medicare, Medicaid and Social Security.

I think the president should focus attention and energy on this debt crisis, rather than on the dubious benefits of a trade war. Getting America's fiscal house in order will make America great again.

Trump's Vitally Important Anti-Poverty Initiative

April 18, 2018

It takes a lot of courage for a president to target almost a quarter of the federal budget for reform in an election year.

But this is exactly what President Trump is doing with his executive order, "Reducing Poverty in America by Promoting Opportunity and Economic Mobility."

We're now spending more than $700 billion per year on low-income assistance, which is more than we are spending on our national defense. And there are plenty of reasons to believe this spending is inefficient, wasteful and counterproductive.

Over the last half-century, some $22 trillion has been spent on anti-poverty programs and yet the percentage of poor in this nation remains unchanged. And it is not only a matter of the percentage staying the same but also that the people and families who are born poor stay that way.

The Better Way report produced by the House speaker's office in 2016 reported that 34 percent of those born and raised in the bottom fifth of the income scale remain there all their lives.

The point has often been made that the greatest charitable gesture is teaching those in need to help themselves.

This principle defines the president's reforms to our anti-poverty programs and spending. Let's make sure that every dollar spent goes to those truly in need and that those dollars are spent to maximize the likelihood that the recipients will get on their feet and become independent, productive, income-earning citizens.

The executive order directs federal agencies to review the some 80 federal anti-poverty programs, consolidate where there is redundancy and overlap, and look to reform by applying the principles of hard work and self-sufficiency.

Needless to say, the usual left-wing megaphones, those that can't tell the difference between compassion and spending billions of other people's dollars, have wasted no time to go on attack.

The headline from the Southern Poverty Law Center screams, "Trump's executive order on work requirements punishes low-income people for being poor."

Calling the executive order "heartless," the SPLC rejects the premise that there are those receiving benefits from these programs who could work but don't.

However, Robert Doar of the American Enterprise Institute reports that there are almost 20 million working-age Americans receiving benefits under Medicaid and food stamps who don't work.

The "Better Way" report notes that "44 percent of work-capable households using federal rental assistance report no annual income from wages."

But it's not just about work requirements.

Vital to this reform project is moving programs out of Washington's grasp and into the administrations at the state and local levels. Assistance programs need humanity and flexibility. This can only be done locally. There's no way an army of bureaucrats in Washington can develop and implement programs for 50 million needy individuals that can properly recognize what unique individuals need to move out of poverty.

Assistance programs need to promote and embody those principles that go hand in hand with prosperity — ownership, investment, savings and personal freedom and responsibility.

According to the Better Way report, almost 10 million Americans have no bank account and another 25 million have an account but get financial services outside of the banking system.

When I was a young woman on welfare, I saw the destruction that occurs when assistance programs penalize work, marriage and saving, as was the case with the Aid to Families with Dependent Children program. Subsequently, this was reformed and transformed with great success to the Temporary Assistance for Needy Families program.

We can't go on spending hundreds of billions of dollars of limited taxpayer funds on programs that may have been conceived with sincerity and compassion but don't work.

President Trump deserves credit for exercising the courage and vision to move to fix what is broken in our anti-poverty programs. It is vital for the poor and vital for the nation.

Who Is Jim Jordan?

April 25, 2018

Ohio Republican Congressman Jim Jordan has confirmed that he is looking to run for House speaker when current Speaker Paul Ryan departs at the end of the year.

This puts Jordan up alongside the other principal candidates, current Majority Leader Kevin McCarthy, R-Calif., whom Ryan has endorsed as his successor, and Majority Whip Steve Scalise, R-La.

Jordan co-founded the House Freedom Caucus in 2015 with eight other conservative Republicans. He explained then that the motivation for founding the caucus was to give "a voice to countless Americans who feel that Washington does not represent them. We support open, accountable and limited government, the Constitution, and the rule of law and policies that promote liberty, safety, and prosperity for all Americans."

The caucus now has more than 30 members and has dug in as a unified bloc fighting for exactly those principles that Jordan articulated at its founding. Most recently, the caucus opposed the $1.3 trillion spending bill passed by congress and urged President Trump to veto it.

In addition to being a fiscal and constitutional conservative, Jordan is also a stalwart pro-life Republican and has been on the front lines fighting to defund Planned Parenthood.

In other words, he stands for what I call the three C's that have been the pillars of American success and greatness.

Christianity, Capitalism and the Constitution.

For this reason, I find the prospect of Jordan running for House speaker of great interest.

In a recent Fox radio interview, Jordan put it best by saying that in order to win, Republicans "have to fight for things. All too often Republicans want to forfeit even before the referee blows the whistle to start the game. ... Let's not forfeit, let's go have the debate."

But it's not just a matter of the fight. It's what the fight is about.

Certainly, in 2015, when the House Freedom Caucus was formed, few would have predicted that Donald Trump would be sitting in the White House today.

Trump's appeal to make America great again spoke to the frustration among many Americans that we've lost touch with our American "exceptionalism." This is the sense that we are not like other nations — that something special and vitally important is going on here. And that this "something" is what has given the nation strength, prosperity and leadership.

Unlike other nations, American identity is about aspiration, not fate. Geography, ethnicity or circumstances of birth do not define America — ideals and principles do.

These ideals define the struggle that is taking place today.

Many want to drag us down to the lowest common denominator when we should be fighting for our highest aspirations.

As we teeter on fiscal and moral bankruptcy, it's the three C's — Christianity, Capitalism and the Constitution — that shine like a lighthouse in the night to guide our ship of state in the direction we need to be headed.

Those who founded the nation, fired up by those ideals, appealed, in the Declaration of Independence, to the "Supreme Judge of the world for the rectitude of our intentions (and) with a firm reliance on the protection of Divine Providence, we mutually pledge to each other our Lives, our Fortunes, and our sacred Honor."

Of course, Jim Jordan faces an uphill struggle to achieve the 218 votes necessary to achieve the House speakership.

But when Jordan says he's ready to fight for it, and that we shouldn't forfeit the game before it starts, he's not just tapping into the dissatisfaction of the nation. He's tapping into what defines the nation and its spirit.

The possibility of bringing the spirit of the Freedom Caucus to lead the House, as Jordan will do, is an exciting development.

Michelle Wolf vs Mike Pence

May 2, 2018

Humor is a good and important thing.

The ability to laugh at life, to laugh at oneself, shows faith, optimism and humility. Laughter in the face of adversity is a sign of a healthy spirit.

In this sense, the annual White House Correspondents' Association dinner was once a positive event.

Poking fun at the highest centers of power in Washington showed that, despite differences of opinion, our commitment to our most fundamental values — particularly our First Amendment protections for freedom of speech and religion — held us together and our sense of nationhood.

But something has happened. The common ground that held us together is shattering.

There was no humor in this year's correspondents' dinner. What pretended to be humor was politicized vulgarity driven by animosity and hate.

The attacks on members of the Trump administration by leftist comedienne Michelle Wolf were shots across a ravine — a ravine that now divides America into two sides that have so little in common, and share so few values, that it is not clear whether our national fabric can withstand the great tension pulling on it.

Wolf called Vice President Pence a "weirdo", saying he "thinks abortion is murder, which, first of all, don't knock it till you try it. And when you do try it really knock it. You know, you got to get that baby out of there."

It interesting that Wolf referred to the humanity in the mother's womb as a "baby." If she thinks the infant is a baby, then she agrees with Mike Pence that abortion is the destruction of a distinct and unique individual.

When we cannot agree as a nation on something so fundamental as the nature and meaning of life, our national unity stands on very shaky ground. This was on display at the correspondents' dinner.

The retiring president of Planned Parenthood, Cecile Richards, is now touring the country promoting her new book in which celebrates her 12 years as head of he nation's largest abortion provider and extolling the virtues of the pro-abortion movement. Not once does she mention, per Alexandra de Sanctis in National Review, that "under her watch Planned Parenthood clinics have performed 3.5 million abortions."

When President Lincoln delivered his second inaugural address, as the Civil War raged, he said, "Both read the same Bible and pray to the same God, and each invokes his aid against the other."

Arguably our national fabric is more damaged today than then, when the nation was torn apart over the issue of slavery.

Not only do the warring sides today not "read the same Bible," but many, probably most, do not read it, care about it, nor share any common thoughts on the existence and nature of our Creator.

According to a new Pew Research report, although 80 percent of Americans say they believe in God, just 56 percent of this 80 percent say they believe in God "as described in Bible."

This means that only 44 percent of all Americans today believe in the God of the Bible.

In a Marist poll of January 2018, 44 percent self-identified as "pro-life" — exactly the same percentage that believe in the God of the Bible.

Perhaps one reason White House Press Secretary Sarah Sanders was able to so graciously hold her composure, despite the vicious attacks directed at her at that maybe final WHCA dinner, was she knew deep inside that Michelle Wolf is the epitome of our nation's great divide, which is not a laughing matter.

Perhaps we should turn again to Lincoln who said that a "nation divided against itself cannot stand." Per his wisdom, we might expect that we will move again to be a nation that reveres life and the God of our Bible. Or maybe we'll continue our descend into the abyss of nihilism.

Draining the Food Stamp Swamp

May 9, 2018

The Supplemental Nutrition Assistance Program is high on the Republican list of programs targeted for reform — and justifiably so.

The program has gone from 17 million enrollees in 2000 to about 43 million today, with outlays up from about $25 billion to more than $70 billion.

The Trump administration's budget submitted last February includes major reforms to the program, designed to save $216 billion over the next decade.

Now the House Agriculture committee has put forth its own reforms as part of the bill reauthorizing the budget of the Department of Agriculture for the next five years.

The problem with the food stamp program is similar to the problem of the other anti-poverty, welfare programs on which we spend almost 25 percent of the federal budget.

That is, what is directed in the spirit of compassion, to provide temporary assistance to those who have fallen on hard times, transforms into a way of life.

As we might expect, food stamp enrollees skyrocketed as the recession set in heavily in 2008. The number of recipients went from approximately 26 million in 2007 to a peak of 47.6 million in 2013. With the economic recovery, the number has dropped off to about 43 million.

The Labor Department now reports that unemployment has fallen to 3.9 percent — the lowest since December 2000. Unemployment peaked during the recession at almost 10 percent. Why, when unemployment has dropped by 61 percent, has the number of food stamp recipients dropped by only 10 percent? The number of recipients is about 17 million higher than before the recession.

The answer is that it's a lot easier to get aid recipients onto a welfare program than get them off.

Although the unemployment rate has dropped dramatically, the employment rate — the percentage of the population over 16 working — is still far below where it was prior to the recession. The latest jobs report shows the employment rate at 60.3 percent. Just prior to the recession in 2007, it was at 63.4 percent. If today's employment rate stood where it was before the recession, there would be 8 million more Americans working.

These 8 million Americans are not sitting on the sidelines just because of food stamps. Disability insurance and other welfare programs also leave the door open to not working.

How to solve this problem? Start with the Reagan rule: "Government is not the solution to our problem; government IS the problem."

The more government we have, the more we make food stamps into the big business it is today. Why do we want corporate lobbyists for firms selling to food stamp EBT cardholders — Walmart, Target, Kroger, and even Amazon — lining the halls of Congress to lobby for these programs?

The Department of Agriculture is proposing that the government provide a food basket instead of cash. There is also the idea that government should manage the nutrition of food stamp recipients. The House bill incentivizes purchases of fruit, vegetables and milk. But do we really want a huge new government bureaucracy buying and packaging food baskets for 40 million enrollees?

I say no. We should not expand government interference in anybody's life.

Instead, the best idea is to expand work requirements for getting benefits. The House bill requires 80 hours of work per month to receive ongoing benefits. This for those 18-49, with no dependents, and parents of school-age children, up to the age of 60. For any new or changed requirements, let's have the states decide.

Government assistance should not be about changing anybody's life. Changing lives should be left to family, friends and private charity.

President Trump and the Israel Test

May 16, 2018

I was privileged to attend the dedication of the new American embassy in Jerusalem on May 14, 2018 — an event of enormous import that will remain with me forever.

I am deeply grateful to Ambassador David Friedman and his wife, Tammy, for inviting me to this historic event.

The United States recognizing Jerusalem as Israel's capital is important not just for the United States and Israel but also for the entire world.

We might start thinking about this by considering the unique relationship between these two countries.

Regardless of how some choose to think about the United States today, the country's founding generation was largely Christian men and women.

Alexis de Tocqueville, author of "Democracy in America," widely deemed to be the most insightful book ever written about the United States, wrote in 1835, "There is no country in the world where the Christian religion retains a greater influence over the souls of men than in America."

Perhaps there is no better example demonstrating this truth, and the deep roots of Christian Americans in the Hebrew Bible, than the inscription on the Liberty Bell from the Book of Leviticus: "Proclaim liberty throughout all the land unto all inhabitants thereof."

The United States and Israel are different from other nations in that both are defined by a creed and by principles.

I would go so far to say that the extraordinary success of both countries springs from these principles.

What are the great principles that can be extracted from the Ten Commandments in the Hebrew Bible?

Reverence for the Lord, reverence for family, reverence for the sanctity of life, reverence for private property and personal responsibility, and a prohibition of envy.

Some surely will say that the United States has strayed so far from these principles that they no longer define the country.

But I travel constantly. I have been in every state of the union. And I have met enough of the many millions of Americans that still subscribe to these truths to know they are still very much alive in America.

And I also believe that the problems that plagued America in the past, and that plague America today, trace to abandonment of these great truths — these great truths rooted in the Hebrew Bible.

I see President Trump's courageous step forward to lead the United States to be the first nation in the world to recognize Jerusalem as the capital of the State of Israel, and to move the United States Embassy to Jerusalem, as implicit recognition that the common ground on which both nations stand is our shared belief in these great and holy truths.

The achievements of the young State of Israel, which celebrates its 70th birthday this year, have been truly awesome.

Writer, social philosopher and investor George Gilder wrote a book called "The Israel Test." What is the Israel Test according to Gilder?

He asks the question: How do you react to those who excel you in innovation, in creativity, in wealth? Do you envy them and feel diminished by them? Or do you admire what they have achieved and try to emulate them?

Those who say the latter pass the Israel Test. According to Gilder, it is the Israel Test that drives today's tensions in the Middle East. I would take it a step further and say that it is the Israel Test that drives the tensions in America.

Gilder says that those who pass the Israel Test tend to become wealthy and peaceful. Those who fail it tend to become poor and violent.

The great principles that join America and Israel are equally true and crucial for all of mankind.

Congratulations to President Trump for helping America pass the Israel Test. Now we wait for the other nations of the world.

A First Step for Prison Reform

May 23, 2018

Recently, I attended the White House Prison Reform Summit.

The fact that both the president and the vice president were at the event indicates the importance that the Trump administration ascribes to this issue.

And statistics quoted by Vice President Pence explain why our existing prison system should trouble us all.

According to the vice president, "Every year, while 650,000 people leave America's prisons, within three years two-thirds of them are arrested again. More than half will be convicted; 40 percent will find themselves back where they started, behind bars. It's a cycle of criminality. It's a cycle of failure."

The encouraging news is that we're seeing a level of bipartisan cooperation on this issue that is rare in Washington these days.

The House Judiciary Committee has just passed a prison reform bill called the First Step Act that is co-sponsored by Republican Doug Collins, R-Ga., and Congressional Black Caucus Democrat Hakeem Jeffries, D-N.Y.

The bill was voted out of committee by a vote of 25-5, with 15 Republicans and 10 Democrats voting for it.

Moderating one of the panels at the White House summit was a former Obama White House advisor, Van Jones, who has come out in support of the First Step Act.

On his Facebook page, Jones called the legislation, "A big win for men and women in federal prison."

The point person in the White House on this issue is presidential advisor Jared Kushner, who deserves much of the credit for raising the profile of the importance prison reform and for recruiting the broad base of support.

The First Step Act establishes new tools for prison management to conduct ongoing risk assessments of each prisoner, evaluating the likelihood of the prisoner recommitting a crime. The profiling also establishes a basis for programs and job training to assist in rehabilitation of these individuals.

Prisoners productively participating in these programs, and showing progress in behavior and attitudes, are rewarded with increased phone time, visits and transfers to facilities closer to their homes and families.

Those achieving a low-risk profile of recidivism may be eligible for at-home confinement or for being transferred to halfway houses for the final period of their sentences.

A group of 121 former federal law enforcement officials have signed a letter urging the passage of the First Step Act.

The list of signatories includes one former U.S. attorney general and five former U.S. deputy attorney generals. And, in the aforementioned spirit of bipartisanship, the list includes Bush Administration Attorney General Michael Mukasey and Mary Jo White, appointed by Barack Obama as chair of the Securities and Exchange Commission and the first and only woman to be U.S. attorney for the Southern District of New York.

Despite the impressive core support for this bill, there is opposition on the left and the right.

Several high-profile Black Caucus Democrats, including Senators Kamala Harris and Cory Booker and Representatives John Lewis and Sheila Jackson Lee, signed a letter in opposition. Also the NAACP opposes the bill.

Complaints include that the risk assessment system is "untested" and that the bill only focuses on prison reform and not sentencing reform.

But the assessment system is not "untested." A good number of states have enacted similar measures with great success. Texas passed similar reforms in 2007, resulting in $3 billion in savings and producing the lowest crime rate in the state in almost 50 years.

There is broad consensus that sentencing reform is also needed. But reform dealing with recidivism is not dependent on this. So why make the politics much more complicated and the probability of passage much lower?

Thoughtful reform to deal with recidivism is both humane and economically sensible. President Trump said he'll sign it if Congress passes it. They should.

Stop Government-Supported Abortion, Family Planning

May 30, 2018

New proposed changes in regulations from the Department of Health and Human Services will close the door on using funds from its Title X family planning program for abortion.

HHS's Office of Population Affairs, which administers this program, is a poster child for ill-conceived government policy. How is it, in our nation that cherishes the ideals of human freedom and dignity, that we're funding government bureaucrats to advise low-income citizens — almost a quarter of these "clients" are black — about how many children they should bring into this world and when?

Despite explicit language in the legislation that created the Title X family program in 1970 prohibiting funding "programs in which abortion is a method of family planning," this directive has been effectively ignored.

HHS reports that 4 million individuals are getting services through this program. However, 1.6 million of them, 40 percent, according to the Guttmacher Institute, are receiving these services at Planned Parenthood clinics.

Given the millions that Planned Parenthood, the nation's largest abortion provider, spends on lobbying and political contributions, its success in keeping the faucet of federal funding of its activities open comes as no surprise.

But now the Trump administration is stepping up to enforce the law, with the positive additional benefit of protecting human life. You might say that our president understands that building a culture of life is a vital part of making America "great again."

The new HHS order requires complete financial and physical separation of Title X funds from abortion activity. No Title X funds can be used for abortion. And abortions cannot be performed in any facility in which programs being funded by Title X are taking place.

Although Title X counselors will be prohibited from discussing abortion as a family planning measure, they can discuss it when a woman has already decided it's what she wants. Then they can provide a list of abortion providers.

But as we think about this, let's consider the bigger question. What is the federal government doing in the family planning business anyway?

The Office of Population Affairs describes, among the activities of its "Family Planning Mission," offering guidance "to assist individuals in determining the number and spacing of their children."

Given that this family planning guidance is targeted to low-income Americans, who happen to be disproportionately black, let's consider what has happened to the black family since the Office of Population Affairs first began.

The budget of the Title X Family Planning program in 1971 was $6 million. Today, it is $286 million dollars, an increase of 50 fold. What have we gotten?

In 1970, 38 percent of black babies were born to unwed mothers. Today it is more than 70 percent.

In 1960, 10 years before the program started, 2 percent of black children lived with an unmarried parent. By 2008, 41 percent did.

In 1960, 61 percent of blacks over the age of 18 were married. By 2008, 32 percent were.

I would suggest that government "family planning" is really an insidious, pernicious kind of racism. It's not about improving the quality of life, but rather it is about discouraging black women, and other poor women, from having children and encouraging them to abort their pregnancies.

The collateral damage has been the collapse of the black family.

This important new HHS proposed rule will take care of the abortion issue.

But we need a broader initiative to get rid of the damaging and wasteful government "family planning" business.

The nation would be better served, particularly at a time of trillion-dollar deficits, to return the $286 million spent on Title X programs to taxpayers.

Black women should be getting their "family planning" guidance from their pastor, not from government bureaucrats.

Will More Blacks Vote Republican?

June 6, 2018

As we churn through primary season, laying the framework for November's elections, we're seeing the emergence of a new face of the Democratic Party — more progressive, more left wing.

The Democratic Party is delivering more candidates around the nation like Stacey Abrams, recently nominated for governor in Georgia. She's unabashedly boilerplate, in-your-face, hard left. Pro-big government, pro-abortion, pro-LGBT rights.

Recent Wall Street Journal/NBC polling shows how the Democratic Party has changed. In 2004, 67 percent of Democrats identified as moderate or conservative and 31 percent identified as liberal. In 2018, we see a shift to the left of 20 points. Forty-seven percent identify as moderate or conservative and 51 percent as liberal.

Amidst all this, what might we expect from blacks, Democrats' most consistent voting bloc? In 14 presidential elections since 1964, Democratic candidates captured an average 88 percent of the black vote. But blacks generally don't fit the new far-left profile.

According to recent data from the Pew Research Center, black Democrats have very little religiously in common with white Democrats. Religious behavior of black Democrats is much more closely aligned with white Republicans.

Forty-seven percent of black Democrats say they attend church at least weekly, compared to 45 percent of white Republicans and 22 percent of white Democrats.

Ninety-two percent of black Protestants say they believe in God as described in the Bible, compared to 70 percent of Republicans and 45 percent of Democrats.

But it's not just religious attitudes that raise questions about black monolithic affinity for the Democratic Party.

In the Pew Religious Landscape study published in 2014, 36 percent of historically black Protestants described themselves as conservative and 24 percent as liberal.

Regarding the role of government, 23 percent of historically black Protestants say they prefer smaller government and fewer services and 70 percent say they prefer larger government and more services.

Regarding government aid to the poor, 27 percent of historically black Protestants say government does more harm than good and 66 percent say government does more good than harm.

You might say that these responses regarding the role of government explain why blacks vote disproportionately for Democrats.

But that's not correct.

The data reported above is for what Pew defines as "historically black protestant" — which, according to Pew, consists of 53 percent of all blacks. However, according to Pew, 79 percent of blacks identify as Christian.

Pew reports in addition to 47 percent of all black Democrats saying they attend church at least once per week, 74 percent say they pray daily, and 76 percent say religion is "very important" in their lives.

So data that Pew reports for historically black Protestants seems to be a reasonably rough sample of black attitudes in general.

When 36 percent identify as conservative, and when 27 percent say government assistance to the poor does more harm than good, yet on average, 88 percent of blacks are voting for Democrats, something is amiss.

Voting Democrat is not written in black genes. From 1936 to 1960, the black vote for the Republican presidential candidate averaged 30 percent. In 1956, 39 percent of blacks voted for Dwight Eisenhower.

Black voting behavior has far reaching implications, as America changes demographically into a country less and less white. In 1980, 88 percent of voters were white. In 2016, 70 percent were. This trend will continue.

In a new Harvard-Harris Poll, 33 percent of blacks say they are now "better off" in their financial situation and 32 percent of blacks approve of the way Trump is handling the economy.

Republican Party outreach to blacks has ratcheted up considerably since the Obama years.

If Republicans can succeed in courting these church-going black Christians, we could see a political realignment in the country that will change profoundly America's political landscape.

Why Can't We Fix Social Security and Medicare?

June 13, 2018

Each year, the trustees of Social Security and Medicare issue their report delivering the news, invariably dismal, about the financial condition of the nation's two largest entitlement programs.

This year, in the report just issued, it's worse than usual.

Last year, the trustees forecast that Social Security and Medicare's hospital insurance would have to start dipping into their trust funds by 2022 and 2023 in order to finance their obligations. They report now that the situation has deteriorated such that both need to start dipping in this year.

The HI trust fund will be depleted by 2026, and Social Security's trust fund will be depleted by 2034.

In the case of Social Security, in 2034, just 16 years away, if no action is taken now, either benefits must be cut by 21 percent or taxes will need to be raised 31 percent, to meet obligations.

Analysts have been writing about the grave fiscal problems of Social Security for years. Yet nothing gets done. Why?

Social Security is the largest spending program in the U.S. budget. Ninety percent of Americans 65 and older get Social Security benefits.

Any government program, once it gets rooted in our culture and Americans start getting benefits, becomes almost impossible to change. President George W. Bush tried to bring fundamental changes to Social Security. He was a Republican president whose party controlled both the Senate and the House. And he still couldn't get to first base.

Social Security was signed into law in 1935 — 83 years ago. Although the scope of the program is much, much bigger today, it's basic structure is exactly the same as it was then. Benefits of retirees are paid for through the payroll taxes of those currently working.

How many businesses today operate exactly like they did 83 years ago — or even 10 years ago? The Dow Jones average, an index of the nation's most influential corporations, has changed 51 times since it was founded.

The reason our economy works is because it is flexible. The world is changing all the time. Businesses are constantly altering their products and the way they do business to accommodate new market realties.

But not so in government programs. And there couldn't be a better reason why we should keep government out of our private lives.

The basic premise of Social Security, and of Medicare, enacted some 33 years after Social Security, was that we could tax the young and working to pay for the retired and elderly.

But in 1950, we had a little over 16 people working for every retiree. Today it is less than 3.

Life expectancy in 1940 for a 65 year old was 14 years. Today it is 20 years.

Meanwhile, we're not having children. Last month, the Centers for Disease Control and Prevention reported that the U.S. fertility, the number of babies birthed for every 1,000 women of childbearing age, was the lowest in history in 2017.

Most Americans think they are entitled to defined Social Security benefits because they paid taxes. It's not true. In a Supreme Court case in 1960, Flemming v. Nestor, the court ruled "A person covered by the Social Security Act has not such a right in old-age benefit payments. ... To engraft upon the Social Security system a concept of 'accrued property rights' would deprive it of the flexibility and boldness in adjustments to every-changing conditions."

This means the government can change your benefits anytime it wants. Who would do business with a company like this?

It's great that President Donald Trump has got our economy steaming ahead again. But as we recover, we need to take on the challenges of Social Security and Medicare.

Do Christians Have a Future in LGBTQ America?

June 20, 2018

In 2014, high-tech executive and CEO of Mozilla Brendan Eich was forced to resign from the company he helped found and build, because he made a $1,000 contribution to support traditional marriage in the California marriage referendum.

According to accounts, Eich was subject to vicious attacks through social media for his contribution in the marriage campaign.

Mozilla chairwoman, Mitchell Baker, observed, "Mozilla believes in both equality and freedom of speech. Equality is necessary for meaningful speech. And you need free speech to fight for equality. Figuring out how to stand for both at the same time can be hard."

That Mozilla's chairwoman could offer such a confused, vacuous explanation for Eich's dismissal sheds light on why the overall state of affairs in the country is such a mess.

Free speech is not about equality. Free speech is about the pursuit of truth. The equality necessary for free speech is equality under the law, where everyone receives equal protection. But when politics is the aim rather than truth, objective law protecting free expression gets flushed, and political operatives, like Baker, determine who lives and who dies.

Two years earlier, Crystal Dixon, a black Christian woman, was fired from her human resources position at the University of Toledo because she penned an op-ed for the local newspaper challenging the proposition that the gay rights movement is a new chapter of the black civil rights movement.

Carefully reasoned discourse — which is what Dixon offered in her fatal op-ed — is not welcome in a politicized society, because the pursuit of truth is no longer relevant. Only behavior consistent with predetermined political ends is.

This slippery slope leads in one direction. Less freedom and more oppression. Exactly what our nation is not supposed to be about.

It shouldn't surprise us, then, that Gay Pride Month has become a time for LGBTQ storm troopers to pursue political enemies. Not much different from the infamous Kristallnacht in Nazi Germany, when Nazi brown shirts took to the streets to smash windows of shops owned by Jews.

Thus among the stories of this Gay Pride Month:

Another high-tech executive, the CEO of Twitter, with an estimated net worth of $5 billion, was forced to offer a social media apology for eating a chicken sandwich in Chick-fil-A. Patronizing a fast-food establishment whose CEO is a devout Christian, with the temerity to have criticized the Supreme Court decision legalizing same-sex marriage, is a high crime in the eyes of the LGBTQ judges and jury.

Russell Berger, chief knowledge officer of CrossFit, was fired for tweeting his support of a company decision to cancel participation of a CrossFit gym in Indianapolis in Gay Pride Month events. Berger, a seminary trained pastor, was perhaps excessively inflammatory because he used the word "sin." If there is any "sin" in today's politicized America, it is to claim that sin, in the biblical sense, exists.

A Muslim Uber driver was fired for asking two lesbian passengers to leave his car after they began kissing and embracing.

Last year, my office in Washington had to temporarily close because of threats when, in a cable TV interview, I equated the LGBTQ rainbow flag to the confederate flag. From my point a view, it's a totally reasonable assertion. As a black American, the Confederate flag communicates to me that I am not welcome. As a Christian American, the rainbow flag communicates to me that I am not welcome.

According to a recent Gallup survey, 41 percent of Americans identify as evangelical Christians. Will the course of events in

LGBTQ-controlled America preclude them from shopping, working, speaking, existing in our nation's public spaces?

The preamble of our constitution says that "We the people" establish this constitution in order to "secure the blessings of liberty to ourselves and our posterity."

The direction of events indicates that "our posterity" has much to be concerned about.

America Divided Against Itself, Again

June 27, 2018

On May 22, 1856, Representative Preston Brooks entered the floor of the United States Senate, approached abolitionist Senator Charles Sumner, and beat the senator with a cane, almost taking his life.

Brooks was provoked by a passionate anti-slavery speech that Sumner had delivered in the Senate three days earlier, in which he assailed Senator Andrew Butler of South Carolina, a relative of Brooks, for his pro-slavery stance.

This sad and gruesome history is related on the website of the U.S. Senate, which concludes saying, "The nation, suffering from the breakdown of reasoned discourse that this event symbolized, tumbled onward toward the catastrophe of the civil war."

We ought to be concerned that again, today, the nation appears to be flirting with this uneasy territory where "reasoned discourse" is breaking down.

The president's press secretary, Sarah Sanders, was asked to leave a restaurant in Lexington, Virginia, where she was having dinner because, well, she works for Donald Trump.

Stephanie Wilkerson, owner of the Red Hen restaurant, said she asked Sanders to depart because "there are moments in time when people need to live their convictions. This appeared to be one."

But what exactly are the "convictions" that Wilkerson was living in this incident? That you refuse to talk, associate, do business with anyone you disagree with? This is America?

A few days before, Homeland Secretary Kirstjen Nielsen was harassed in a D.C. restaurant and then at her Northern Virginia home.

Longtime Congressional Black Caucus member Maxine Waters followed, calling for all out warfare on the Trump administration.

"If you see anybody from that Cabinet in a restaurant, in a department store, at a gasoline station, you get out and you create a crowd and you push back on them, and you tell them they're not welcome anymore, anywhere," Waters told a crowd in Los Angeles.

According to the vision statement of Waters' Congressional Black Caucus Foundation: "We envision a world in which all communities have an equal voice in public policy through leadership cultivation, economic empowerment, and civic engagement."

Another dose of liberal hypocrisy.

"Reasoned discourse" can take place only between parties who share the same values and a similar worldview.

This is what broke down in America in the 1850s and brought the nation to a horrible civil war. Reasoned discourse is not possible between someone who thinks it is acceptable for one race to be enslaved to another and someone who finds this abhorrent.

President Lincoln reached into the Gospel of Matthew and prophetically observed, "A house divided against itself cannot stand."

America in 2018 is becoming again a house divided.

The world views of liberals and conservatives, Democrats and Republicans, secular humanists and Christians, regarding what America is about, regarding what life is about, are so entirely different that all common ground seems lost and we appear to have arrived again to the "breakdown of reasoned discourse."

Half the country is on one page and half on another. We can't seem to talk to each other, let alone respect each other anymore.

Certainly, I am not predicting another civil war. But I am predicting that the kind of civil discourse that is essential for a country like ours to function as intended is becoming increasingly impossible and something will have to give.

Florida's Republican Attorney General Pam Bondi required a police escort to protect her from screaming thugs while exiting a movie theater in Tampa, Florida.

White House adviser Stephen Miller was called a "fascist" while eating in a Mexican restaurant in Washington.

We may not be in a hot war. But we *are* in a cold war.

The election of Donald Trump was about pushback.

He himself is regularly criticized for lack of civility. But maybe this is why he won. He understands that today, this is the game.

The Demagoguery of
Alexandria Ocasio-Cortez

July 4, 2018

Now that Alexandria Ocasio-Cortez has rocketed into the national spotlight as result of her stunning primary victory over incumbent Democrat Joe Crowley in New York's 14th Congressional District, what's the message for national politics?

How did this young woman, who has never held or run for political office, beat a 10-term incumbent by 15 points, whose funds were, by some estimates, 15 times greater than hers?

Even more so when she is a declared socialist, wants government health care for all, tuition-free colleges, is an outspoken advocate for the LGBTQ agenda, and an aggressive critic of Israel.

According to Ocasio-Cortez, "There are a lot of districts in this country that are like New York 14, that have changed a lot in the last 20 years, but their representation has not."

But this district is very unique and not at all representative of most congressional districts around the country.

According to the Census Bureau, it breaks down demographically as 22 percent white, 50 percent Hispanic, 9 percent black and 16 percent Asian.

In addition, 45.8 percent in this district are foreign-born and 67.8 percent report that they speak a language other than English at home.

To connect the dots, Ocasio-Cortez is telling us and wants us to believe that a district that is so-called majority minority, with almost half of the population foreign-born and the majority of whom don't speak English at home, should have a socialist representing them in Congress.

The problem with Joe Crowley, according to Ocasio-Cortez, was that although he is a liberal, he's not far enough left. He's not a socialist, and therefore out of touch with the Hispanics, blacks and Asians in this district.

Sorry, it's not my idea of good representation to tell constituents that their lives will be improved if the United States becomes more like the failed, problematic places that many of them, and their forebears, left to come here.

Consider Puerto Rico, where Ocasio-Cortez traces her roots, which is an economic basket case, as result of the same kind of big government ideas that Ocasio-Cortez is telling the constituents of New York 14 they need for a better life.

According to recent congressional testimony of Desmond Lachman of the America Enterprise Institute, "Over the past decade, the Puerto Rican economy has shrunk 10 percent while more than 10 percent of its population has migrated to the mainland. At the same time its unemployment rate remains over 12 percent and barely 40 percent of its population participates in the labor market.

"Puerto Rico's public finances have become seriously compromised in large measure due to years of economic mismanagement. This has led to a large public deficit, an excessive public debt to GNP ratio, and a very large amount of unfunded pension liabilities."

While Ocasio-Cortez has gained voters by promising everyone a free lunch paid for by the U.S. government, the Congressional Budget Office is issuing warnings of the same problems in our nation — huge deficits and crushing national debt — that has crippled Puerto Rico.

Although New York 14 is very different from the average American congressional district, the demographic changes of our nation are headed in that direction.

Per the Census Bureau, over 50 percent of Americans today age 5 and below are not white.

We need to be running candidates in every district around America who understand and are committed to the principles of freedom and limited government that created the great nation to which so many want to come.

This is what our minorities and youth need to be hearing.

Unfortunately, too often they are being abandoned to the distortions of left-wing demagogues like Ocasio-Cortez.

We need candidates that are as clear and passionate about the truth of freedom as Alexandria Ocasio-Cortez is about the lies of socialism.

Abortion and the Constitution

July 11, 2018

As we enter into what surely will be another contentious confirmation process for a new Supreme Court justice, let's consider underlying realities that deeply divide us and make it so hard to agree about how our Constitution should be interpreted and applied.

The Declaration of Independence lays the groundwork for us.

It tells us that all men are endowed by their Creator "with certain unalienable rights, that among these are life, liberty, and the pursuit of happiness. — That to secure these rights governments are instituted among men."

The important news here, if you accept the founding document of our nation, is that human rights are not created by government. They precede it. The point of government is to build a fence around and protect these rights — these truths — articulated in the Declaration.

Regarding life, the Declaration tells us that the role of government is to protect it.

This explains the rancor surrounding Roe v. Wade and legal abortion that is becoming center stage to our court confirmation deliberations.

Legal abortion is, at its core, about whether unborn children should be included in what we consider mankind. If yes, they must be protected, like all life.

The "pro-life" movement is clear on this. The unborn child is living and must be protected.

Where's the other side coming from?

Most telling is from then-candidate Barack Obama, who told Pastor Rick Warren, in response to Warren's question, at what point "does a baby get human rights?" that the answer "is above my pay grade."

President Obama was an aggressive advocate for abortion and was the first sitting president to address the annual meeting of Planned Parenthood, where he concluded his remarks with "God Bless You."

He was comfortable invoking the blessings of God for the nation's largest abortion provider despite his candor that he has no idea whether abortion means taking human life.

Recently, Maine Republican Senator Susan Collins expressed dismay at border security policies that separate children from their parents. Collins called this "traumatizing to children, who are innocent victims, and it is contrary to our values in this country."

At the same time, Collins says she will not support a Supreme Court nominee "who demonstrated hostility to Roe v. Wade."

I ask Collins, is the unborn child, who has a heartbeat and can feel pain, not also an innocent victim? Does Collins not find this violence on life also "contrary to our values in this country"?

Perhaps Collins finds taking a position on whether the unborn child is human life, like Obama, above her pay grade.

Collins, and others, tell us that Roe v. Wade is "settled law" and therefore now intrinsically part of American life. To overturn it, they say, would create intolerable disruptions. I reject this bogus idea.

If you believe the unborn child is living, that life must be protected under the U.S. Constitution.

Several years ago, Lord Jonathan Sacks, former Chief Rabbi of the United Kingdom, spoke at the Humanum colloquium on complementarity at the Vatican. He began his remarks, which received a standing ovation, saying he would speak about "the most beautiful idea in the history of civilization: the idea of the love that brings new life into the world. ... Life begins when male and female meet and embrace."

As we move forward to confirm a new Supreme Court justice, let's remember that although our Constitution was constructed by men, it was designed to protect and preserve principles from a higher place.

Abortion is a symptom of, not the cause of, the tensions and confusion in our nation. Our real problem is the abandonment of our society to the crass, gross ideas of an empty and false materialism that can only take us to oblivion.

Jim Jordan, Brett Kavanaugh and Journalism By Innuendo

July 18, 2018

First it was Republican Congressman Jim Jordan. Now it's Supreme Court nominee Brett Kavanaugh.

These men are considered guilty by association for being in proximity of wrongdoing that took place almost 30 years ago.

Allegedly, Jordan took no action as a young assistant wrestling coach regarding sexual misconduct of the team's doctor.

And Kavanaugh was a law clerk for a judge later accused of sexual harassment.

There will be questions to Kavanaugh during his confirmations hearings, which will relegate these absurd insinuations to the trash where they belong.

But Jordan is an influential conservative congressman, and he is being hurt.

Why is it so easy for the media to inflict damage at what appears to be so little cost to them?

I'm reminded of the Duke University lacrosse team rape-case fiasco in 2006, where a corrupt prosecutor with an agenda and an all too willing left-wing press and university administration were ready to convict young men — with no facts.

It was just too beautiful a story for the left: young white athletes raping a black woman that they hired to strip at their team party house.

Except it didn't happen. But the team coach was fired; the university suspended the team and cancelled the playing season. The players were tried and convicted in the press, and 88 members of the Duke University faculty signed a letter carried in the university newspaper essentially confirming the guilt of the players and the alleged crime.

How can we not be thinking about this case with these horrible and unsubstantiated allegations surrounding Jordan, who to all who know him is a man of impeccable character and standards?

Where's the reporting on those who knew Jordan from this time and who substantiate his claim that he didn't know what was going on?

James Freeman of The Wall Street Journal provides the sought-after responsible journalism on this issue. He reports that midway in Jordan's coaching career, he recruited his cousin, a high school wrestling star, to Ohio State. Freeman quotes Jordan's cousin that the possibility that Jordan would recruit him to a place where he would "be threatened by a sexual predator is so outside the realm of possibility that it's laughable."

Further, as Freeman reports, astonishingly the law firm Ohio State has hired to investigate this, Perkins Coie, is the same firm hired by Hillary Clinton's campaign to develop the dossier on Donald Trump.

Is it an accident that Jim Jordan, who is going after the FBI like an attack dog and is now contending for House speaker, is somehow now being exposed to this character assassination?

Sally Quinn, a former columnist and widow of The Washington Post's Watergate-era editor Ben Bradlee, recently wrote in Politico about her late husband's commitment to truth in journalism. But today the Post is part of the journalism-by-innuendo cesspool. A recent Post column by a staffer of former Democrat Senate leader Harry Reid advises probing what law clerk Brett Kavanaugh might have known about sexual harassment by his then-boss Judge Alex Kozinski 27 years ago, as a strategy to block Kavanaugh's confirmation.

We know the left bias of the press. According to the Center for Public Integrity, 96 percent of political contributions in 2016 identified from journalists went to Hillary Clinton. According to a 2013 survey, journalists identifying as Democratic outnumber those identifying as Republican 4 to 1. In a survey published in 2016 of 40 top universities, Democrats in journalism departments outnumber Republicans 20 to 1.

But our problem with the press is less about politics than integrity. The ease with which flimsy insinuation is published as information, insinuation that can cause serious damage to a person of quality, is something that should deeply concern every American. We should not tolerate it.

Senate Should Pass the First Step Act

July 25, 2018

It is rare these days in Washington to see bipartisan support for anything, let alone for a major issue with far reaching implications for the nation.

This is why the bipartisan passage in the House, 360-59, of the First Step Act to reform our federal prisons is such big news. The 360 "yes" votes included 134 Democrats.

The bill focuses on improving the management of our existing federal prison population and the abysmal statistics regarding recidivism — the likelihood that an ex-con will wind up back in prison. Data point to 68 percent of those released within three years, and 77 percent within five years, will be back behind bars.

The bill allocates funds for education, drug treatment and job skills training programs. Risk assessment procedures will be utilized to assess each inmate on the likelihood of recidivism, and programs will be available for inmates to get credits for early release and for the opportunity to serve time remaining at home or a halfway house.

The bill also requires more humane treatment of women inmates who are pregnant and give birth in prison.

You would think that Senate Republicans would be rolling out the red carpet for the First Step Act, particularly given that it's an initiative that started in the White House.

Unfortunately, that's not happening. Senate Judiciary Committee Chairman Chuck Grassley is not moving to embrace this bill because it doesn't including sentencing reform.

With all due respect to Senator Grassley, he's making a mistake. And as a result he's hurting his party and his country.

In all my years working in public policy, one lesson I have learned is that it is an invitation for failure to try to deal with a complex issue, one having a number of separate components, in a single huge, complicated piece of legislation. The result is either no action or a sweeping — and bad — law.

This is exactly why we get nowhere with fixing our health care system and with dealing with immigration.

Clearly, we have an enormous criminal justice problem in our country.

It is a moral and fiscal disaster that our free nation has, per capita, more people sitting in prison than any nation in the world. According to World Prison Brief, the U.S. has 655 individuals in prison per 100,000 in population, making our incarceration rate highest in the world.

Everyone agrees we have a criminal justice problem. But like so many other areas, there is a woeful lack of agreement about what is causing the problem and how to solve it.

And this brings us back to the incredible bipartisan passage of the First Step Act.

Senate Majority Leader McConnell and Senator Grassley should see this as an opportunity for the Republican-controlled Congress to show it can act decisively on a major national problem. Holding up prison reform to add on the complex issue of sentencing reform will result in what I said above: either nothing will happen or we'll get one big unworkable bill.

Furthermore, prison reform has major racial implications. Blacks, who constitute 12 percent of the population, make up 33 percent of the prison population. Hispanics, who constitute 16 percent of the general population, make up 23 percent of the prison population.

It's no accident that the NAACP opposes the bill. Or that Obama administration Attorney General Eric Holder wrote in The Washington Post against it. Or that two very politically ambitious black Democratic Senators, Kamala Harris and Cory Booker, oppose it.

Passage of the First Step Act would show that Republicans care and can help a large part of minority America in distress. Black Democrats don't want this to happen.

Senate Republicans must keep an eye on retaining control in November. They should get on the same page with the White House and the House and pass the First Step Act.

The Trump, GOP Economic Recovery

August 1, 2018

When I read that the economy is growing strongly, it makes me happy.

But in politics, good news is not enough. You have to decide who gets credit for it.

President Ronald Reagan, no ordinary politician, kept a plaque on his desk that said, "There is no limit to what a man can do or where he can go if he does not mind who gets the credit."

Nevertheless, a good deal of the discussion surrounding the news that the economy grew hugely in the second quarter this year — 4.1 percent — has been about how much credit President Donald Trump deserves.

Paul Krugman, the very left-wing Nobel prize-winning economist, for whom there is nothing Trump can do that is good for the American people, dismissed this great economic news in his New York Times column, calling it a "nothingburger."

I think it's more than a "nothingburger" to the many finding their way back into the workforce because of a brisk economy growing at a pace we haven't seen in years.

The Wall Street Journal now reports that "Americans looking to land a first job or break into a dream career face their best odds of success in years."

According to the report, companies trying to hire in a labor market that is now very tight are loosening the requirements that they once sought in job applicants.

Thirty percent of job postings now require, at minimum, a college degree. This is down from 34 percent from 2012. Now, 23 percent of entry-level jobs require three or more years of work experience. This is down from 29 percent in 2012.

The drop in work requirements puts 1.2 million jobs "in closer reach to more applicants," per The Wall Street Journal story.

Now this same Krugman wrote a piece a few weeks back in The New York Times: "The G.O.P.'s War on the Poor."

Krugman is unhappy about Republican proposals to add work requirements to welfare programs like Medicaid. Which, I think, is a great idea.

But the point here is that the best answer for those on welfare who can work is a job. And that the best anti-poverty program is a growing, robust economy.

More jobs and opportunity is the "nothingburger" that is now being served up to millions of Americans.

Now there's the question about how much credit Trump and the Republican Congress can take for this.

We know what Krugman thinks. But there are also distinguished economists who share with Trump the conviction that the economy is recovering because of the tax cuts and deregulation measures that have been put in place over the last year and a half.

It is worth looking at the Economic Freedom of the World Index, published annually by the Fraser Institute in Vancouver, Canada. The index measures economic freedom in 159 countries around the world, using 42 different parameters.

The index is important because it correlates extremely strongly with economic growth. Countries that score the best grow the fastest.

In 2000, the U.S. was No. 4 out of 159 countries. By 2014, the U.S. dropped to No. 14. Scores regarding the size of our government, our legal system and business regulation all deteriorated. This correlated with the slowdown in growth and the very slow economic recovery.

These are all the areas that Trump is fixing. So it's no surprise that the economy is recovering.

I don't have a Nobel Prize in economics. But I'm ready to give President Trump and Republicans the credit. Contrary to a GOP "war on the poor," I'd say, with an abundance of new jobs, and historically low unemployment rates for blacks and Hispanics, the

GOP is leading a new economic renaissance for the poor and all working Americans.

Lessons from Apple at a Trillion Dollars

August 8, 2018

Apple has become the first U.S. company in history to attain a trillion-dollar valuation. Here are a few thoughts about the relevance of this to our country today.

The story of Apple is the story of Steve Jobs. He co-founded the company in 1976 at the age 21, was fired from this same company at age 30, and then returned 11 years later, as it teetered on the edge of bankruptcy, to restore it and set it on the path it has arrived to today.

First thing to think about is that Jobs was born in 1955. His biological mother, an unwed graduate student, gave birth and arranged for his adoption. This was 18 years before abortion became legal in America by way of Roe v. Wade.

If Jobs was conceived 18 years later, or if Roe v. Wade had become law of the land 18 years earlier, there is some chance that there never would have been a Steve Jobs. The life that would have become Steve Jobs could have been another in the vast sea of abortion statistics. There would be no Macs, iPods or iPhones.

Another thing worth contemplating is the vitality of freedom and capitalism, not just to us, but also to the whole world.

By the end of the third quarter of 1997, when Jobs had returned to Apple, the company had lost more than a billion dollars and, by his estimate, they were within 90 days of insolvency.

Jobs reviewed Apple's whole product line, and out of 15 products, he eliminated 11. Three-thousand workers were immediately laid off.

By 1998, Apple was once again profitable.

The key point is not just that Steve Jobs was a unique, driven and extraordinarily gifted entrepreneur. Also, he was free to do what he thought needed to be done.

Once he regained control of the company, he took full responsibility to assess the situation and took immediate steps to fix what he saw as broken.

Consider, in contrast, another trillion-dollar story.

The trillion-dollar budget deficits that the U.S. government faces now and into the near future.

Washington is filled with think tanks with all kinds of bright people with Ph.D.s analyzing and writing reports recommending what needs to be done to fix things.

But these reports then go to politicians who can't, or won't, take action.

We've got all kinds of recommendations, but no one can take charge, assume total responsibility, decide what to do, and do it.

Welfare programs and entitlement programs, many of which were developed 50 to 80 years ago, clearly don't work well and need to be either redesigned or eliminated, go on, year after year.

It's the nature of the beast. We can't change government. What we can do is limit its size and growth and maximize our private sector where freedom and capitalism can work.

It's important to think about this at a time when we're hearing so much, particularly from our young people, about how wonderful things would be with more government, more socialism.

Steve Jobs was committed to innovation — to "evolving, moving, refining" — all the time. More of our young people should be thinking about that while tweeting about socialism on their iPhones.

Surely, these sentiments motivated many when they voted for a businessman to be in the White House. They wanted a tough guy who could do what needed to be done and say, "You're fired!" to those not performing.

But it's a lot harder in Washington. Most cannot be fired. There are very few things that can be accomplished alone.

So the two lessons I take from Apple at a trillion dollars:

The vital importance and uniqueness of every human life. And the vital importance of freedom and capitalism.

Urban Violence Begins in Broken Homes

August 15, 2018

The Chicago Tribune reported a big drop in violence in Chicago this past weekend. Forty people were shot.

This down from the weekend before, when 74 were shot.

The Tribune's Steve Chapman rejects what he calls the "popular myth, cynically promoted by Trump and other outside critics" that Chicago is an "exceptionally dangerous city."

Yes, 674 people were murdered last year in Chicago, more than in New York City and Los Angeles combined. But that is much better than 1991 when, says Chapman, 920 were murdered, and the 674 killed in 2017 was down 15 percent from 2016.

Whether or not we call this violence "exceptional," it is certainly unacceptable. It should concern us all, particularly it's racial characteristics.

As Chapman notes, "Chicago's crime problem is concentrated in a small number of poor, blighted, mostly African-American neighborhoods."

He continues, "Those areas owe their plight largely to a sordid history of systematic, deliberate racial discrimination and violence, endemic poverty, and official neglect over the years."

For sure, misguided government policies have contributed to this sad state of affairs. But these policies were supposed to help these communities, not destroy them.

Policies, such as excessive taxation and government housing, that have fostered indifferent absentee landlords and crime-ridden neighborhoods.

If there is any "deliberate racial discrimination" that drives violence and crime in black urban areas, it is the racial discrimination of the left. It is the racial discrimination of identity politics, which promote the idea that different ethnicities should live under different rules and receive special treatment.

Let's recall that the unfairness that blacks had to deal with in America's history was unequal treatment under the law. This is what needed to be fixed, and this is what was fixed in the Civil Rights Act in 1964.

The problem was that liberals wanted to use their agenda not to fix the law but to change the country. And in the name of racial fairness, the era of big activist government, financed with oceans of taxpayer funds, was born.

But government can't fix anybody's life. It can only make sure that the law protecting life, liberty and property is applied fairly and equally.

The beginning of big activist government fostered the demise of personal responsibility.

The perpetrators, and victims, of violence in Chicago and other urban areas are largely young black men. They mostly come from homes with no father and from communities where this reality is the rule rather than the exception.

Making a child is not hard to do. Raising a child and conveying the values and rules that make for a successful life and responsible adulthood is. Particularly now that popular culture largely dismisses these truths. And in black communities, politics and media is dominated by the left, whose message for them is that life is unfair because of racism and the answer is big government.

According to recent data from the Pew Research Center, 36 percent of black children under 18, compared to 74 percent of white children under 18, live in a household with married parents.

And according to Pew, 30 percent of households headed by a single mother, 17 percent of households headed by a single father, 16 percent of households headed by an unmarried couple, and 8 percent of households headed by a married couple are poor.

Data from the Cook County Department of Health show that, in suburban Cook County and in Cook County under Department of Health jurisdiction, in 2016, 86 percent of babies born to black women between 18-29 were born out of wedlock.

President Donald Trump is doing his job. We have robust economic growth that we haven't seen in years, with unemployment rates at record lows.

Black leaders need to start doing their job and convey that marriage, work, education and personal responsibility are the only things that will fix black America.

King's Dream Still Relevant Today

August 22, 2018

We are approaching the 55th anniversary of Dr. Martin Luther King Jr.'s famous "I Have a Dream" speech, delivered Aug. 28, 1963, in Washington, D.C.

Reading through the speech, it's hard not to be in awe, like those who stood and heard King then, by the greatness and truth of his words.

He captured with precision what America is about, what was wrong then, and what needed to be done.

And because timeless truth is what made that speech great, it is still relevant to today's considerable challenges.

This was not the speech of a political activist. This was a sermon of a pastor, enlightened and inspired by his God, to fix what was broken in America and lead us all to better world.

I see three great messages from King's speech that are important to grasp and apply today.

First, King said that they were in Washington that day to cash in and "demand the riches of freedom and the security of justice."

Second, he communicated that freedom and justice are of divine origin, as he quoted from the prophet Isaiah.

And third, of particular relevance and importance today, was King's appeal to not drink "from the cup of bitterness and hatred" and to "conduct our struggle on the high plane of dignity and discipline."

I doubt that there is anyone that would not recognize the widespread failure in today's America to honor this last appeal for civility. The level on which our national discourse is now taking place is disappointing.

And I would relate the widespread decline of mutual respect to the extent to which we have purged the presence of God — as vital today as it was to King's message in 1968 — from our nation's public spaces.

Looking over the last 55 years, there have been failures but also great successes regarding black life in America.

I think the successes tie to the extent to which black life has followed the principles that King laid out in the "I Have a Dream" speech, and the failures tie to departures from those principles.

A new study from the American Enterprise Institute in Washington, D.C., captures this.

The study, "Black Men Making It In America: The engines of economic success for black men in America," reports the good news that 57 percent of black men today have made it into America's middle class or higher, compared to 38 percent in 1960.

And that "the share of black men who are poor has fallen from 41 percent in 1960 to 18 percent in 2016."

What are the "engines of success" for black men, according to the study? In addition to higher education and full-time work, the study ties three institutions to successful black men — military service, church attendance and marriage.

Fifty-four percent of black men who served in the military versus 45 percent who did not reached the middle class at midlife. Fifty-three percent of those who attended church at a young age, compared with 43 percent who did not, reached the middle class. And 70 percent of married black men, compared with 20 percent of never-married and 44 percent of divorced black men, are in the middle class.

Another critical factor is what the study calls "individual agency." This is the sense of personal responsibility for and control over one's life. Fifty-two percent of black men with a high sense of "agency," compared with 44 percent without, achieved at least middle-class status by age 50.

King did not lead a revolution. He led a national wake-up call. He pushed the nation to take responsibility for what it was and is — a free nation under God.

And the justice he sought was that government secure life, liberty and property, in the name of freedom, for "all of God's children."

Republicans Can, Must Keep
Control in Midterms

August 29, 2018

Recent polls and surveys are delivering, at best, mixed news for Republicans regarding the upcoming midterm elections.

The good news is that prospects have turned positive for Republicans to win Senate seats currently held by Democrats in Florida, New Jersey and Wisconsin.

But looking for good news in the House is a bigger challenge. Probability assessments from various sources give Republicans a 25 to 50 percent chance of keeping control of the House.

A survey from Pew Research points to greater engagement from Democratic voters — by measures such as participating in rallies and making political contributions — than Republicans.

So despite pockets of good news, on balance there's a lot of pessimism about Republican prospects in the midterms.

All this pessimism brings to mind the famous response of the American General Kincaid when, during the Battle of the Bulge, the Germans suggested he surrender. His response: "Nuts!"

The news about America is the best it has been in years.

The economy is growing at a pace that many said would never happen again.

The face of our federal judiciary — from district courts to the U.S. Supreme Court, as result of conservative appointments made over the last year and a half — has never been more encouraging for those who believe that law and fidelity to the Constitution matter.

Internationally, from Europe and the Middle East to the U.N. and China, America once again stands its ground and does not concede

on the core principles that make our nation exceptional and great —
human freedom and dignity and the right to private property.

Amidst all this, why anyone would want to turn the House back
to a welfare state run by Nancy Pelosi and Maxine Waters, with
sclerotic growth and moral relativism, is a mystery.

Democrats are pouring in funds, feverishly targeting key
Republican districts. And, of course, they're getting plenty of help
from the left-wing propaganda machine that is the mainstream
media.

And this same propaganda machine continues to push out the lie
that Republicans are hostile to minorities.

But blacks see and feel the truth. Record low black and Hispanic
unemployment rates show the robust economy is reaching all
Americans.

The NAACP's own polling shows black approval for President
Trump at 21 percent, more than three times higher than the
percentage of blacks that voted for him in 2016. A Rasmussen poll
shows black approval for Trump at an incredible 36 percent.

Which brings me to a remarkable young man, John James, who,
with the endorsement of President Trump, won the Republican
primary for the Senate in Michigan. James is a 37-year-old black
conservative. A graduate of West Point, he served in Iraq where he
piloted Apache helicopters, and he now runs his family business in
Michigan.

James will run against establishment Democrat Debbie
Stabenow, who is looking to capture her fourth term in the Senate.
Recent polls show Stabenow with a 15-point advantage. But the race
has not yet started, and James could capture this seat. Trump was the
first Republican to win in Michigan since 1988, and his victory was
heavily driven by white working-class voters who were tired of the
Democrat status quo.

No state was more heavily hit by the assault on manufacturing,
by the financial collapse, and by Democratic mismanagement, than
Michigan. A Republican governor and a focus on prudent fiscal
management have turned things around. The Census Bureau reported
in 2017 that for the first time since 2001 more people moved into
Michigan than left.

John James, with his conservative appeal and sterling credentials, is an exciting new face of the Republican Party and could be one of the great surprises and upsets of 2018.

This is a time for Republicans to dig in, fight like never before, and say "nuts" to the naysayers. Republicans can, and must, hold both Houses in 2018.

The Flawed Retrospectives on John McCain

September 5, 2018

The passing of Senator John McCain was marked by a sea of eulogies mourning the end of an era of civility and compromise.

What has happened, they ask, to those noble, bipartisan days of yesteryear, and how have we descended into today's crude and primitive tribalism?

I read this stuff and wonder where I was during those wonderfully tranquil, civil days gone by.

Maybe because I am black, I see American history through a different lens. The truth as I read it in our history, and as I have experienced it in my life, is that America has always been a battlefield of ideas and interests.

What is unique about our great country is not the absence of conflict but rather that it occurs openly and honestly — and that we survive it, time and again, with our national institutions intact.

So it is not confrontation that bothers me. It is dishonesty. And I see a lot of the latter in what I have been reading regarding the alleged era of civility that has come to a close with the passing of Senator McCain.

One of the hymns played at McCain's memorial services at the National Cathedral was "The Battle Hymn of the Republic." It was reported to be one of McCain's favorites.

"The Battle Hymn of the Republic" was, of course, a hymn, a march, of the Civil War, during which some 750,000 Americans lost their lives.

It was a war no one wanted. In Abraham Lincoln's words, "Both parties deprecated war, but one of them would make war rather than let the nation survive, the other would accept war rather than let it perish, and the war came."

The disagreement on core principles was too great. "And the war came."

Lincoln himself was gunned down in the end.

The last line of the last speech given by Martin Luther King Jr., the night before his assassination in Memphis, Tennessee, was from "The Battle Hymn of the Republic": "Mine eyes have seen the glory of the coming of the Lord."

America is a battlefield because America is about truth, and truth is something only won in struggle.

Let's take a look at how our nation has changed since John McCain's plane was shot down in Vietnam in 1967.

In 1967, abortion was still illegal in America. Since abortion on demand became legal through Roe v. Wade in 1973, more than 60 million of our babies have been destroyed.

In 1967, 10 percent of our babies were born to unwed mothers. Today it is more than 40 percent.

In 1967, about 8 percent of white adults over the age of 25 and 9 percent of black adults of the age of 25 had never been married. By 2012, 16 percent of white adults and 36 percent of black adults had never been married.

In 1967, no one would have dreamed that in America the sacred and holy institution of marriage could be anything other than the bond between one man and one woman.

The 1960s marked the beginning of the moral decline of our nation and the flowering of the civil rights movement. One pushed moral ambiguity; the other pushed for moral clarity.

The stretch from the 1960s to today, during which John McCain served in Washington, was about struggle. What might be taken as a time of bipartisanship and compromise was instead more about morality and politics.

"The real crisis we face today," President Reagan said in his famous speech to the National Association of Evangelicals in 1983, "is a spiritual one: at root it is a test of moral will and faith."

This is our struggle. Let's be honest and unapologetic about it.

School Disciplinary Policies Must Be Local

September 12, 2018

The Trump administration is considering rescinding a Dear Colleague Letter, sent to public school administrators nationwide in 2014, which provided guidelines regarding school discipline policies consistent with Title VI of the Civil Rights Act.

According to Title VI, racial discrimination at institutions receiving federal funds is illegal.

The letter was sent by the Obama administration Department of Justice's civil rights division and the Department of Education's office for civil rights.

The point of the letter was, according to then-Secretary of Education Arne Duncan, to provide "information on how schools and districts can meet their legal obligations to administer student discipline without discrimination on race, color, or national origin."

Sounds reasonable enough. But a closer look reveals that these were far more than guidelines. Behind the scenes, the Obama administration's Department of Education used the DCL to aggressively launch investigations to assure that school districts implemented these guidelines, which constituted a highly questionable departure from what civil rights law requires.

The DCL informed school officials that they would be investigating more than disciplinary *policies* applied variably across racial lines. Now, uniformly constructed and applied disciplinary policies would be viewed as noncompliant if they produce disparate *results*.

One doesn't need to be a constitutional or civil rights law scholar to see this as a problem.

And, in fact, when current Supreme Court Justice Clarence Thomas was assistant secretary for civil rights at the Department of Education in 1981, his guidelines were quite clear that discrimination constituted different rules or different application of those rules between races — not uniform rules and applications that produce disparate results.

The Obama administration's DCL guidelines overturned and replaced Thomas' guidelines.

As documented by scholar Max Eden of the Manhattan Institute, the whole point was to change the role of the Department of Education's office for civil rights from an entity that monitors compliance with the law to an entity that decides what policies and procedures school administrators should be following — and to find them noncompliant if out of line.

Given that we're talking about the threat of cutting off federal funds, can there be any question that public school officials became more interested in the wants of federal government than what the best policies were locally?

According to Eden, from 2009 to 2017, "at least 350 school districts — serving nearly 10 million children, or about one-fifth of all public elementary and secondary schools students in the U.S. — were investigated for the express purpose of coercing districts into changing their disciplinary policies."

Eden continues, "According to (then-Secretary of Education) Duncan, societal ills such as poverty, broken families, and neighborhood crime have little effect on student behavior. Rather, racism among teachers and administrators is responsible for the fact that black students are more than three times as likely as white students to be suspended."

President Trump's Department of Education's office for civil rights should withdraw and rescind this 2014 Dear Colleague Letter.

Can it really be that hard to appreciate that all discipline problems of black children may not be rooted in racism? Every child is unique. Personal challenges can only be handled personally and intimately, and thus should only involve local school officials, the child, parents and their supportive community.

At minimum, let's restore the Department of Education's civil rights job to what it should be — monitoring compliance with the law instead of deciding how local educators should run their schools.

More local flexibility and mobility through vouchers or other parental choice platforms may be exactly what students need, not an overhaul of our entire public schooling apparatus.

Feinstein v. Kavanaugh

September 19, 2018

While questioning Supreme Court nominee Brett Kavanaugh about abortion during his Senate confirmation hearings, Senator Dianne Feinstein grossly misstated statistics about abortion deaths before Roe v. Wade.

"In the 1950s and 1960s, two decades before Roe, deaths from illegal abortions in this country ran between 200,000 and 1.2 million. That's according to the Guttmacher Institute."

The Guttmacher Institute has very close ties to the abortion lobby, but even their numbers proved Feinstein way off base.

The Guttmacher study actually reported 200,000 to 1.2 million as the number of procedures. Regarding actual deaths, in 1965, for example, there were 200, according to Guttmacher.

When corrected, Feinstein was dismissive of the gravity of her error. "So, a lot of women died in that period," she demurred.

Feinstein's distortion of data points to the agenda driving this new discussion from the left to derail the Kavanaugh vote by any means necessary.

Nothing, certainly not facts, will get in the way of their attempts to control the courts, regardless of any collateral damage done to the reputation of an upstanding and decent man.

Thus we can understand the sudden emergence of Christine Blasey Ford and her claim that Brett Kavanaugh sexually assaulted her in 1982, when she was 15 and he was 17.

As reported in The Washington Post, Ford, a vocal progressive and pro-Democrat donor, wrote to Feinstein, the ranking Democrat on the Senate Judiciary Committee, describing the incident but requesting anonymity, in July.

Apparently, Feinstein was so moved to keep the letter anonymous that she buried the contents as well as the identity of the author.

Per reports, Feinstein did not ask Kavanaugh about this in her interview with him prior to the hearings. Nor did she question Kavanaugh about it during the hearings.

Suddenly, two months after Feinstein received Ford's letter, she announced she had information about Kavanaugh that she reported to the FBI.

Then a story revealing the contents of Ford's letter appeared in the press. Days later, Ford concluded her "civic responsibility" compelled her to shed anonymity and step forward, armed with a polygraph test corroborating her story and a seasoned, progressive legal advisor.

How can anyone take this seriously?

Even liberals should concede that in America one is innocent until proven guilty. Particularly with 36-year-old allegations that are impossible to corroborate.

Kavanaugh has had a long, distinguished career, serving as counsel in the White House and for the last 12 years as a federal district appeals court judge. Along with this, he has undergone a half-dozen FBI background checks, with no irregularities arising.

This is now standard fare for Democrats. When they perceive that our constitutionally defined machinery of government is not serving their far-left interests, they reach into the "dirty tricks" bag and pull out racist or sexual accusations to derail things.

This is exactly the swamp in Washington that President Trump was elected to drain.

If Feinstein thought Ford's accusations had teeth, then she had two months to vet them. It is a travesty to our system of government and justice to now interrupt the progress of Kavanaugh's confirmation with these tenuous claims. Feinstein had her chance.

It is transparent that this is about Democrats wishing to cause a delay until after November, opening the door for a new, progressive nominee, should Democrats gain control of congress.

Nothing prevents Democrats from continuing to investigate Kavanaugh after he is confirmed — if they so wish.

The abuse that concerns me now is the abuse of our system of government by devious progressive political operatives.

It is imperative that Republicans show leadership now, before the election in November, and move forward immediately to vote on Judge Kavanaugh's nomination.

Kavanaugh Show Will Help Republicans in November

September 26, 2018

A new report from Gallup should sober up those expecting a "blue wave" in the November elections.

According to this recently released report, the percent of Americans saying they have a "favorable" view of Republicans now stands at 45 percent, up from 36 percent. Favorability for Democrats stands at 44 percent, exactly where it was last September.

This is the highest favorability for Republicans since January 2011, when it stood at 47 percent just after Republicans gained control of Congress in the 2010 midterm elections.

Of particular interest are large gains for Republican favorability among men — now at 50 percent, up from 37 percent a year ago — and middle-income households ($30,000 to $74,999), now at 49 percent, up from 36 percent a year ago.

Republican favorability has even increased among women — 40 percent now compared to 35 percent last September.

It makes complete sense that Republican favorability among voters should be surging and that Democrat favorability should be languishing.

How could the shameful carnival that Democrats have created around the confirmation of Judge Brett Kavanaugh not hurt them?

One of the most common mistakes made today is to think that political process — that is, democracy — is what makes us free. No, it is law.

It is law that protects life, liberty and property. Rule of law, which is honored, respected and applied equally to every citizen regardless of race, gender and anything else, must stand above political bias. This assures our society is free and just.

The absence of equally applied law is what tore our nation apart in the 1850s, with the acceptance of slavery and the infamous Dred Scott decision, denying African-Americans legal status as citizens.

The whole point of the 14th Amendment, enacted after the Civil War, was to guarantee every American due process and equal protection under the law.

But with this show around Kavanaugh's confirmation, the Democratic Party has unmasked itself as a party whose only interest is in a left-wing political agenda, not the law.

It is exactly why Democrats see conservative judges, like Kavanaugh, who take the Constitution seriously, as a mortal threat. Democrats want politics and their agenda, not law.

Hence, an outstanding and honorable man's good name and reputation is being besmirched with unsubstantiated and tenuous claims.

The long-accepted tradition that the burden of proof is upon the accuser, not the accused, is being thrown to the trash bin.

It should be of particular concern to blacks and women that we live in a nation in which law stands above politics. Blacks, because this is what the civil rights movement was about. Women, because this is not just about themselves and their daughters but equally about their husbands and sons.

The economy is booming. In recent days, stock indexes have reached new highs and, as The Wall Street Journal reports, new claims for jobless benefits have "hit a half-century low."

The National Federation of Independent Business reports record high optimism and hiring plans among small businesses, the main job generators in our economy.

The Republican Senate has now confirmed 68 conservative judges to the federal bench — with 125 to go.

And every federal department administrating anti-poverty funds - which constitute one-quarter of the federal budget — must follow an executive order from President Donald Trump to become more efficient.

Yes, it's true that generally the president's party loses congressional seats in midterm elections. However, in 2014,

Democrats lost only 13 House seats in the midterms, despite Barack Obama's 44 percent approval, which isn't far from where Trump stands today.

Republicans need to stand firm with the truth on Kavanaugh. That plus the great economic news in our nation will take them over the finish line in November.

Pro-Abortion Left vs. Kavanaugh

October 3, 2018

I've been writing for years about the depth of the culture war taking place in America. I've done so with trepidation, with knowledge that without resolution, culture wars can turn into physical wars.

It happened once in America. Can it happen again?

The first major violent confrontation between citizens came about as result of the question of slavery. The country's founders included the proposition in our founding that all men are created equal. We lived for many years untrue to this proposition, and that unfaithfulness in spirit lead to war.

Similarly today, we are deeply divided over the meaning and relevance of our founding proposition that we are endowed by our Creator with rights to life, liberty and the pursuit of happiness.

The core point of contention is abortion. The nation is divided right down the middle between those that believe the unborn must be protected like all life and those that relegate the unborn to some other category, giving women free license to destroy what others understand to be humanity.

Although there are as yet no armed battles, other kinds of violence are now disrupting our national life.

We see it in the confirmation process of Judge Brett Kavanaugh.

The efforts by liberals to derail Kavanaugh's nomination are driven by fear that he could be a threat to Roe v. Wade. It's all about abortion.

The battle cry we have heard and are hearing is that those who see it essential to move forward with Kavanaugh's confirmation "don't care about women."

No matter how many women step forward to attest to Kavanaugh's decency, liberals are convinced that he doesn't care about women. For them, anyone not supporting legal abortion on demand doesn't care about women. Conversely, for them, "caring" about women means unrestricted legal abortion.

Dr. Martin Luther King Jr wrote in his famous "Letter from a Birmingham Jail": "A just law is a man-made code that squares with the moral law, or the law of God. An unjust law is a law that is out of harmony with the moral law."

King, in this letter, justified civil disobedience and breaking laws that are unjust.

Those disrupting the process to confirm Kavanaugh, by any means possible, are similarly motivated. But the key and massive difference is that the law they see as unjust, one which would protect life in the womb, is exactly what King defined as a just law — "one that squares with the moral law, or the law of God."

So any sense of morality in law, or the procedures to carry out the law, has no meaning for those driven by keeping abortion legal. For them, the law is not rooted in moral traditions. Rather, it's what they make up for their own convenience.

It's why the war against Judge Kavanaugh, his family and all those that support him, is so unprincipled and vicious. Those who feel they don't need any higher authority for truth, that they can make it all up based on personal predilections, have no moral code limiting what they'll do. They are capable of anything, which is what we are witnessing now.

If there is a vital takeaway from the horror we have witnessed in this confirmation process, it is to appreciate the depth of the culture war in which our nation finds itself.

There is no easy way out. We are going to have to decide who we are as Americans, what values define us, and what code characterizes the law under which we live.

Will it be the moral code of a nation under God or the synthetic, arbitrary standards of a nation of secular humanism?

Will Kavanaugh Realign Racial Politics?

October 10, 2019

With nerves still raw from the wrenching confirmation process of now Supreme Court Associate Justice Brett Kavanaugh, speculation whirls regarding what the political implications will be.

Worth considering is where the racial lines will be drawn.

Among the more aggressive voices from the Democratic side of the Senate Judiciary Committee fighting to derail the Kavanaugh nomination, were two of the most prominent black Democrats in the country — Cory Booker of New Jersey and Kamala Harris of California.

The presidential ambitions of both are known and transparent, and they clearly viewed these hearings as a platform to advance their national personae.

What might these two black senators tell us about the direction of racial politics in the country?

Both, in my view, point to a core redefining of the black presence in the Democratic Party.

Although African-Americans have been a reliable voting base for the Democratic Party since the mid-'60s, blacks have never been defined by the liberalism of that party, particular in recent years.

One point of deep division is religion.

African-Americans are among the most religious demographics in the country and self-identified Democrats are among the least.

According to Gallup, 51 percent of Republicans self-identify as "highly religious" compared with 33 percent of Democrats.

Whereas 41 percent of Americans describe themselves as "born again" or evangelical, 61 of blacks do.

Thirty-three percent of Americans say they attend church once per week. But 61 percent of blacks do.

African-Americans sympathizing with activist government, rather than with core liberal values, has always been a major factor in their identification with the Democratic Party.

But the movement of Democrats farther left, highlighted by the divisiveness of the Kavanaugh hearings, could be a watershed in racial politics.

Booker and Harris are rooted more in Democratic Party progressivism than the traditional concerns of black Democrats.

Both continue to hype the uncorroborated claims against Kavanaugh, despite an FBI follow-up investigation verifying that there is not one witness that corroborates Christine Blasey Ford's allegations.

Booker is talking about about pursuing Kavanaugh's impeachment. Harris is going on about the alleged denial of "justice for sexual assault survivors."

However, Kavanaugh's confirmation process was never about justice for sexual assault survivors. It was about carrying out the law based on facts rather than unsubstantiated claims by interested parties.

Former presidential advisor and Senator Daniel Patrick Moynihan famously said, "Everyone is entitled to their own opinion, but not their own facts."

Kavanaugh survived the contentious confirmation hearing because there were no facts leveled against him, just accusations. Booker and Harris, by focusing on these unsubstantiated claims, demonstrate that progressives don't care about the facts.

It is this kind of perversion of justice, displacing facts with prejudice and claims, that has historically been used to persecute blacks — particularly sexual assault claims leveled against black men.

More blacks are beginning to understand that what serves their interests is a nation of law, a nation of moral integrity, a nation in which government protects individuals rather persecuting them based on prejudicial thinking.

In brief, what I call the three Cs — Christianity, capitalism and the Constitution.

More black Americans are waking up to the truth that political opportunism, so prominently on display now by Sens. Cory Booker and Kamala Harris, is exactly what they don't need.

A booming economy and unemployment claims at historic lows are the result of a nation of law, not a nation of politics. The Supreme Court is on a new track, with a solid conservative majority in place.

This is good news for all Americans. And more and more black Americans are beginning to understand this.

Midterms About Future of American Freedom

October 17, 2018

According to the Pew Research Center, 66 percent of those supporting Democratic candidates and 18 percent of those supporting Republican candidates say, "If a person is rich, it is because he or she had more advantages in life than most other people."

This from a new Pew survey of Democratic and Republican voters, going into the midterm elections.

There couldn't be a bolder picture of the deep division between Democrats and Republicans regarding what America is about.

Consider the richest man in America, Jeff Bezos. He's the founder and chairman of Amazon and is worth well over 100 billion dollars, depending on where the stock market ends up on any given day.

Did Bezos achieve this phenomenal wealth because he had "more advantages in life than most other people"?

Bezos was born to a teenage mother and a father who was an alcoholic. The marriage lasted one year.

When Bezos was 4 years old, his mother married Mike Bezos, a Cuban immigrant who arrived in the USA when he was 15.

Per accounts of the family, Bezos' stepfather was an ambitious, hardworking man. But there is nothing in the story that would suggest something extraordinary or some kind of formula for producing one of richest men in the world.

In 1994, as the new internet technology emerged, Bezos saw the potential, quit a good job at an investment firm, and founded Amazon.

According to Forbes Magazine, which annually publishes a list of the 400 wealthiest Americans, 69 percent are self-made.

How about Oprah Winfrey, worth $2.8 billion, according to Forbes? She was born poor, on a farm in Mississippi, to unmarried parents, and raised by her grandmother.

No, the American story is not about one's life being determined by circumstances. Individuals have free choice and must ultimately take responsibility for the course of their own lives.

Sometimes I wonder how many Americans have actually read our Declaration of Independence. "Governments are instituted among men," according to our founding document, "to secure these rights" of life, liberty and the pursuit of happiness.

Government, in the American vision, exists to protect individual freedom, not to decide who should have what and invade individual private space, capture private property and income, and redistribute it to others based on what politicians think.

Not surprisingly, according to the same Pew survey, 68 percent of those supporting Democratic candidates, versus 29 percent of those supporting Republican candidates, believe "if a person is poor, it is more due to circumstances beyond his or her control."

The survey contains a list of issues, all consistently showing that Democrats want government to run our lives and that Republicans believe in freedom. There is only one place that Democrats want personal freedom. They want freedom for women to kill their unborn children.

That's the picture and what we're looking at in the upcoming midterms. Are we going to have a free country, as envisioned by our nation's founders? Will we have a nation that respects the sanctity of life and the right and responsibility of each individual to choose their personal destiny?

Or will we live in a nation where our destiny is determined by a political class and political connections?

The more we spend, the more we grow and expand government programs, the more we tax our citizens and accumulate massive government debt to finance it all, the harder it will be to turn back.

Local elections have national implications. Voting for Democrats should be understood as a conscious decision to relinquish our freedom as envisioned by America's founders and for which we have been fighting for almost two and half centuries.

It's Democrats Who Shred American Values

October 24, 2018

While campaign stumping in Las Vegas, former Vice President Joe Biden said that American values are being "shredded" by President Donald Trump.

According to Biden, the United States was founded "on an idea, an American idea, basic fundamental decency, and it's being shredded."

Considering Biden's professed interest in American values and first principles, it's worth recalling the words of George Washington in his Farewell Address.

"Of all the dispositions and habits which lead to political prosperity, religion and morality are indispensible supports," observed our first president. He continued: "Where is the security for property, for reputation, for life, if the sense of religious obligation desert the oaths which are the instruments of investigation in courts of justice? And let us with caution indulge the supposition that morality can be maintained without religion."

In these few words, Washington warned against everything that Biden's Democratic Party has become. Washington said that we should never buy into the illusion that we can have a lawful society that protects life, liberty and property if our laws are not rooted in immutable eternal principles.

Abandoning these basic truths has caused this "shredding" of American values. And that is exactly what Democrats have done and want to continue to do.

This was on grand display during the confirmation hearings of Judge Brett Kavanaugh, where Democrats were so driven to destroy his nomination that they had no reservations in destroying the man or his family along with it.

A society without objective truth is a society with no respect for facts. So it would make sense that a man could be convicted by allegation, by uncorroborated claims, as Democrats tried to do to Kavanaugh.

The Trump administration is attempting to turn our nation from the suicidal path of relativism and subjective truth on which Biden and his party has taken us.

Currently, for instance, the Department of Health and Human Services is moving to re-write the Obama administration's legal definition of sex, which turned gender definition into a matter of personal whim rather than biological fact.

"Sex means a person's status as a male or female based on immutable biological traits identifiable by or before birth..." according to the re-write being proposed by HHS.

Such clarity is vital considering laws like Title IX of the civil rights act that protect against gender discrimination. What could gender discrimination mean if gender has no factual basis and is just something that individuals make up?

The detachment of Democrats from factual reality, and hence from any truth-based morality, has led to the collapse of the traditional American family and to destructive social experimentation. This social experimentation, rooted in relativism, leads inevitability to human tragedy. And blacks and minorities always wind up paying the dearest price.

Consider the recent horror story of a white lesbian couple who adopted six black children, with the tragic result of the mother deliberating driving over a cliff at 90 miles an hour, killing them all. It is unconscionable that along with breaking the traditional definition of marriage and family, we now allow children to be adopted into untraditional, at best experimental, circumstances.

It is Biden's Democratic Party that has shredded American values. Not Donald Trump.

It follows that the party that doesn't care about facts and truth cannot understand or care about diversity in education, and hence supports teachers' unions over parental choice.

And it is Joe Biden's party that thinks the welfare state, rather than personal morality, virtue and responsibility, leads people to financial stability.

Traditional American values — family, education, work — are critical to our future.

It's why voters should choose Republicans in November.

Fake News Threatens Our National Health and Wealth

October 31, 2018

President Donald Trump was right to tweet out: "There is great anger in our Country caused in part by inaccurate, and even fraudulent reporting of the news. The Fake News Media, the true enemy of the people, must stop the open & obvious hostility & report the news honestly and fairly. That will do much to put out the flame..."

He's right.

I open to the opinion section of The Washington Post and find the following headlines:

"Trump has stoked the fears of the Bowerses (the Pittsburg synagogue murderer) among us."

"Fox News and the rest of the right-wing media can't escape responsibility."

"Trump's America is not a safe place for Jews."

All on one opinion page in one day.

As I wrote recently, we learned in the confirmation hearing of Judge Brett Kavanaugh that Democrats are no longer pretending to care about facts. An outstanding American was almost destroyed by uncorroborated allegations.

I was in Jerusalem earlier this year and participated in ceremonies in which the embassy of the United States was moved to Israel's capital, Jerusalem.

A sense of awe, tied to the history of the moment and the bold leadership of Trump, permeated the proceedings. Certainly no one in attendance would question that the Jewish people have no greater friend than this president, who did what no other American president had the courage and conviction to do.

In June 2015, a year and half before the Trump presidency, a young white supremacist entered a black church in Charleston, South Carolina, and murdered nine black Christians.

"It is unfathomable that somebody in today's society could walk into a church while people are having a prayer meeting and take their lives," said Charleston's police chief.

Then-South Carolina Governor Nikki Haley provided extraordinary leadership following the incident, sharing her genuine grief with South Carolinians and all Americans. She took the bold step as a Republican governor to remove the confederate flag from the grounds of South Carolina's capitol.

Haley understood that the best way to fight evil is by identifying evil for what it is and fighting it not with politics but with virtue.

For the last two years, Haley has demonstrated similar leadership by principle as Trump's United Nations ambassador.

A story on CNN Wire, reported nine days before Election Day, leads with the headline: "'Voting while black': How activists are racing to create a midterm 'black wave.'"

According to the report, "A growing network of African-American political groups are laboring to build a lasting political clout for African-Americans, especially in the South, where more than half of nation's black residents live."

The article focuses on three black Democrats running for governorships in Georgia, Florida and Maryland.

You would think that being black and political meant only electing far-left, progressive Democrats. Totally ignored are exciting and potentially paradigm-changing elections involving black Republicans.

John James, a black Republican running for the Senate in Michigan against three-term liberal Democrat Debbie Stabenow, doesn't exist for these CNN writers. James is a conservative Christian, a West Point graduate who flew Apache helicopters in Iraq, and he now runs his family business in Detroit.

James is real news and hence a non-item for the "fake news" dealers whose interest is peddling progressivism, not truth.

Differences of opinion are healthy and vital in a free country. National unity and mutual respect are not threatened by differences of opinion but by the destruction of our first principles that guarantee every America equal protection of life, liberty and property.

Politics of identity, special interests or moral relativism rely on feeding the vulnerable fake news rather than truth. Our national health and prosperity are endangered when the truth is lost to politics.

This is what voters should be thinking about between now and Nov. 6.

The Battle to MAGA Continues

November 7, 2018

America's founders demonstrated that government is art, not science. The secret is in balance.

Biennial congressional elections strike the right balance for the need for stability with the need for change.

Midterm elections take place with the continuity of a sitting president. Whoever is in the White House will continue in this position for another two years, regardless of the outcome of midterms.

By the time you read this, we'll know whether the new Congress will be red or blue. But I know now that the day after the elections, Donald Trump will still be president.

And I know that whatever happens, Trump will stay focused, as he must, on the agenda that he campaigned on and the vision he articulated in his inaugural address.

His commitment to those ideas and principles took him across the nation to insert his persona and agenda into the campaign. As we approach the two-year mark of this presidency, facts bear out that the nation is turning around and "Make America Great Again" is more than a slogan.

We are a deeply divided country with a culture war raging. The battle for steering the country's direction will continue. This election just determines the army that the general in the White House will have to support him in the fight.

Personally, I spent the last month in eight different states, making the case for what is at stake. I spent Election Day in my district, walking precincts and making phone calls to help my candidate of choice in a race for an open seat.

Trump has made it fashionable again to be a patriot, to feel proud to be an American because our nation is indeed unique and exceptional.

The other side has distorted this message of nationalism, claiming it disrespects our diversity and individual differences. Nothing could be further from the truth.

The fact that I am black Christian woman does not contradict my patriotism. I am an American who needs the freedom that only this nation can provide to realize my full potential. This is true for every American. And it is only possible in a nation that is free and informed by eternal truths.

The changes we see in realizing the MAGA goals are tangible and palpable.

Internationally, Trump's idea that the best way to influence the world is to recapture our national greatness is working.

He has shaken up the United Nations and is creating new realities in Asia, South America and the Middle East.

Despite warnings against his bold move to recognize Jerusalem as Israel's capital, Trump did it. And miracles are occurring throughout the Middle East. Israel and Persian Gulf States are forming new relationships that once were unheard of. Israel, for the first time, competed in an international Judo competition in Abu Dhabi, won a gold medal, and the Israeli national anthem was played in this Arab country.

Economically, the economy is back on the path to growth. Black and Hispanic unemployment are at all-time lows, and even high school dropouts are finding work as result of the new opportunities.

Constitutionally, the GOP Senate has confirmed 68 conservative judges, with 125 left to go.

Fiscally, every federal department getting anti-poverty money (one-fourth of the federal budget) is under Executive Order to cut spending and strike new efficiencies.

We need secure borders. Terrorists from the Middle East could penetrate Central and South America, looking to cross our borders under the guise of being refugees.

The bottom line is we must stay the course and continue to help this president get the nation's work done.

We must continue the fight for freedom and personal responsibility and national destiny through MAGA.

Republican Opportunity
With Young Blacks

November 14, 2018

Buried in the mounds of data fleshing out what happened in the midterm elections is an interesting take on blacks.

Nationwide data on black voting in this election cycle do not point to much change. Various polls over recent months seemed to indicate that blacks were starting to warm up to Republicans and President Donald Trump. But blacks went 90 percent for Democrats and 8 percent for Republicans. Pretty much business as usual.

However, digging down, we find something interesting.

Blacks ages 18 to 29 voted 82 percent for Democrats and 14 percent for Republicans. That seems to point to change taking place among young blacks.

Lending support to this conclusion is the fact that in the 2014 midterms, 18-to-29-year-old blacks voted in concert with the overall average, 88 percent for Democrats and 11 percent for Republicans.

Either we have a fluke in this year's midterms or some kind of change in political thinking is taking hold among young African-Americans.

I think there is good reason to believe the latter. Of course, where it goes depends on how Republicans choose to think about and handle the situation.

Adding to this curiosity is something else of interest. The inclination to vote Republican as a function of age is the complete reverse for blacks as it is for whites.

Younger blacks vote Republican at higher percentages than older blacks. Younger whites vote Republican at lower percentages than older whites.

Compared with the 14 percent of 18-to-29-year-old blacks who voted Republican in the midterms, 6.5 percent of blacks 45 or older voted Republican.

Compared with the 43 percent of 18-to-29-year-old whites who voted Republican, 58.5 percent of whites 45 or older voted Republican.

How might we understand this?

According to the Federal Reserve, as of 2016 median black household income was $35,400, and median black household net worth was $17,600. Contrast that with $61,200 median income and $171,000 median net worth for whites.

After all these years of government programs to help low-income Americans, African-Americans, on average, are not catching up.

Perhaps the message is sinking in to young blacks that what they need is more freedom and the kind of growing economy that goes with it.

They are seeing firsthand the results in the economic recovery that has taken place over the past two years. There were over 650,000 more blacks working last month than there were in October 2017. Compared with the average monthly numbers of 2016, there were over 1.3 million more blacks working.

According to reports that have been rolling out during this recovery, the boom has created a tight job market, which has created new opportunities for previously unemployable lower-end workers. This has meant new opportunities for young blacks.

Young white voters — who, on average, come from higher-income homes and have a higher chance of getting help in starting out from their parents — seem to be likelier to buy into the big-government and social justice mindset than their parents and grandparents.

Republicans should highlight for young blacks the critical importance of capitalism and a free economy for upward mobility. However, they also need to inform them that the same Federal Reserve report showing large gaps in income and wealth between blacks and whites also shows 61 percent of white households as having a married couple or romantic partners, compared with 37 percent of black households.

The message is that wealth is created through freedom and family.

President Trump won in 2016 by flipping states that were blue to red by very thin margins.

Florida, for example, with 29 electoral votes, which Trump won by a margin of about 1 percentage point, will be critical in 2020. We see now the elections there for senator and governor at razor-thin margins.

Republicans should target African-Americans in Florida and other swing states with the message of upward mobility. It could make all the difference in 2020.

A Lesson in Racial Politics from Florida

November 21, 2018

Now that, finally, the elections in Florida have reached a conclusion, there are lessons worth learning. One is on the subject of race.

There was a fateful anomaly in racial voting in the governor's race between Democrat Andrew Gillum and Republican Rick DeSantis, now Florida's governor-elect.

Given that Gillum, formerly mayor of Tallahassee, was running to become the first black governor of Florida, we might have expected black enthusiasm for his candidacy on the order of the waves of black enthusiasm for the presidential candidacy of Barak Obama.

But it didn't happen.

Gillum received a lower percentage of the black vote than did Democrat Senator Bill Nelson, who lost to Rick Scott in the senate race.

White Democrat Nelson got 90 percent of the black vote and Republican Scott got 10 percent.

In the governor's race, black Democrat Gillum got 86 percent of the black vote, four percentage points less than Nelson, against Republican DeSantis' 14 percent.

Given the razor-thin margins, that difference in black support meant a lot.

When Gillum finally conceded the election, he was behind by 33,683 votes. Each 1 percent of the black vote equated to about 10,000 votes. So if Gillum had received 90 percent of the black vote, as did Bill Nelson, rather than 86 percent, he could well have had another 40,000 votes, which would have been his margin of victory.

Forty thousand votes is about 35 percent of the 112,911 votes by which Donald Trump won Florida in 2016. It's 55 percent of the 73,189 votes by which Barack Obama won Florida in 2012.

So understanding why Gillum received 4 percentage points less of the black vote than Nelson, and why DeSantis received 4 percentage points more of the black vote than Scott could make all the difference in what presidential candidate wins Florida in 2020.

Adding to the puzzle is the fact that racial politics played a high profile and nasty role in the Gillum-DeSantis contest.

Gillum was aggressive in his allegations of racism against DeSantis. "Now, I'm not calling Mr. DeSantis a racist, I'm simply saying the racists believe he is racist," he said. He accused DeSantis of getting financial support from white supremacist groups and speaking at their events.

DeSantis, a conservative former Republican congressman, made his support of Trump a centerpiece of his campaign, and President Trump campaigned for him in Florida.

So how does this all compute?

One convincing line of speculation is that DeSantis campaigned aggressively on parental choice in education and keeping in place and expanding the tax-credit scholarship program enacted under Governor Jeb Bush. Gillum campaigned on closing down the program, which empowers parents to use these funds to send their children to charter and private schools.

Polls consistently show that blacks support parental choice in education. And for good reason. Black children are disproportionately trapped in failing, violent public schools. Black parents want alternatives for their kids.

Gillum took the left-wing party line on education choice, against the sentiments of black constituents. This could have made all the difference.

The lesson here is that blacks care about issues more than they care about skin color.

It's an important lesson for Republicans going forward. They need to tune in to black concerns, which often are not the same as those of whites, and explain how the best solutions for those concerns are the conservative solutions.

In addition to education, this means addressing issues such as housing, urban violence and prison reform.

The governor's race in Florida gives us good reason to believe that a more aggressive, targeted effort by Republicans in reaching out to minority communities could make all the difference in the outcome of the presidential election in 2020.

When Democrats Win, Freedom Loses

November 28, 2018

The headlines about the incoming 116th Congress scream that our representation has never been so "young," so "blue," so "diverse."

If diversity is about how people look, this Congress is very diverse. It's a fact that there has never been so great a number of representatives who are women and people of color.

There are 124 women, 55 blacks, 43 Latinos and 15 Asians.

But if diversity means diversity of thought, it's practically nonexistent.

Of the 124 women, 105 are Democrats. Of the 55 blacks, all are Democrats. Of the 43 Latinos, 34 are Democrats. Of the 15 Asians, 14 are Democrats.

The celebration about alleged diversity is really a celebration of one, uniform voice on the left, dressed in different colors, calling in unison for moving America further toward socialism and secular humanism.

All the politics of today's Democratic Party, which is as far left as it has ever been, is about how people look and where they come from. Once we called this prejudice or stereotyping. Now we call it progressivism.

This is anything but Martin Luther King's famous dream that his children would one day be judged by "the content of their character and not the color of their skin."

It takes a certain blindness to miss the irony in these politicians of the left, who call for honoring and empowering individuals, and choose to do this by making them less free. They claim to enhance individual dignity by expanding government to dictate our health care, how we save and retire, our relationship with our employer, how and what we can say to others and what they can say to us, and just about every detail of our private lives and decisions.

How has it become so lost in our country that the way we dignify individuals is by believing in them, by granting them freedom to take responsibility for their own life?

In this election, Republicans won a national majority only from white voters. Hispanics voted 69 percent for Democrats; blacks, 90 percent; and Asians, 77 percent.

Minority Americans have bought the lie that personal freedom is not in their interest — that government should run their lives. This is meaningful to us all because they represent the growth demographics of the nation.

According to recent analysis from the Brookings Institution, white America will be in the minority by 2045. However by 2027, just eight years from now, the majority of Americans 29 and under will be non-white.

The socialists, the secular humanists, know time is on their side. It's a waiting game for them.

The new Democrat House has only one thing in mind — biding its time to inflict maximum damage on President Donald Trump in order to lay the groundwork for whomever they nominate for president in 2020. So expect a very noisy two years.

What can Republicans do? Get far more aggressive in reaching into these minority communities about what losing or gaining freedom will mean to them. Republicans have a very important story to tell that is not reaching these communities.

Countries that are not free don't grow, because all the activity is about transferring wealth — not creating it.

The progressive politics of blame, dependence and envy make the well-connected rich and keep impoverished people poor. It's why over the last 50 years, many black politicians have gotten wealthy while the gap in average household income between whites and blacks is 50 percent greater today than it was in 1970.

Republicans and all Americans who care about bequeathing a free nation to their children and grandchildren need to think long and hard about how to communicate the importance of freedom to

Americans of color. It's our only hope of not losing our country to the left forever.

Thinking About What's Right in America

December 5, 2018

Amid this holiday season of reflection, I'm thinking about America's future.

A new poll from Gallup serves up some sobering data regarding how young Americans feel about their country.

Gallup asked the question, "Do you think the U.S. has a unique character that makes it the greatest country in the world, or don't you think so?"

Eighty percent said "yes," America is the greatest country, in 2010 and 78 percent said yes in 2018.

However, among 18- to 34-year-olds, 80 percent said yes in 2010 but this dropped by 18 percentage points in 2018 to 62 percent.

It's troubling to think that now 4 out of 10 young Americans do not see their nation as exceptional and the greatest in the world.

Maybe there is a sense creeping into our youth that America is no longer the land of opportunity that it once was.

In a 2017 Pew Research Global Attitudes and Trends survey, only 37 percent of Americans said they believed so when asked, "When children today grow up, will they be better off financially than their parents?" This compared with 82 percent in China (in 2016), 69 percent in Chile and 50 percent in Israel.

According to recent data from the Brookings Institution, just 50 percent of those born in 1984 earn more than their parents, compared with 61 percent of those born in 1970 and 79 percent of those born in 1950.

But if America's youth are losing a sense that this is a land of dreams, this sentiment doesn't seem to be shared by the million immigrants who arrive in the U.S. every year.

According to a new study by the National Foundation for American Policy, 55 percent of privately held startup companies in the U.S. now worth more than a billion dollars were started by immigrants from 25 different countries.

The study reports that the collective value of these firms founded by immigrants is $248 billion and each company employs an average of 1,200 people.

Most of these immigrant entrepreneurs came to the U.S. to study as international students and chose to stay and become citizens. However, some arrived as refugees and were sponsored by family members.

This all tells me that America is still a land of dreams and opportunity. Are there things wrong with this country? Certainly. But there still is plenty that is right.

Those who choose to uproot from nations all over the world to come here and start their lives anew are interested in what is right, not what is wrong.

I like this quote from former TV personality Art Linkletter, who observed, "Things turn out the best for the people who make the best of the way things turn out."

There's an important point here. Success is not just about one's circumstances, but also what is happening inside of each individual — one's character.

The holidays are a good time to think about this.

I suggest two things. First, let's look at what is right about America. And second, let every American ask themselves if they truly believe they are the best they can be, and if not, why not?

Let's each take personal responsibility to make ourselves and our country as great as possible and stop thinking that it's others and circumstances that block our path.

I think the nation would soar, even with the things that are wrong, if all Americans got out of bed each morning with the sense that what happens to them is not because of anything but what they themselves choose to do. And, if at the same time, we related to ourselves and everyone else as created in the image of God.

We all would discover how much power each of us has and we all would discover how great America is, because it is free.

Family Breakdown Explains Social Unrest

December 12, 2018

As France is gripped by civil disorder, many commentators identify, quite correctly, as the culprit the outsized burden that France's bloated welfare state places on its citizens.

According a recent report from the Organization for Economic Cooperation and Development, the highest tax burden in the industrialized world is in France — 46.1 percent of GDP.

In the United States, it is 27 percent, which includes taxes paid at all levels of government — federal, state and local.

Welfare state spending in France is 32 percent of GDP, almost double that of the U.S., meaning that 1 out of every 3 dollars generated by the French economy is captured by the government and redistributed into social/welfare spending.

But let's recall that all this government was put in place in the name of making life better for France's citizens.

There's plenty of analysis regarding the French situation, as there is in our own country, about how to streamline and reform government programs and deliver the same quality of services at a reduced spending and tax burden on citizens.

But these discussions invariably fail to look at the full scope of human reality at play.

The vast expansion of the welfare state, both in Europe and in the United States, occurred in tandem with a weakening of the family. And weakening of the family generally occurs in an environment of weakening of religion.

When I speak and tell audiences that today 4 in 10 babies in the United States are born to unwed mothers, compared with less than 1 in 10 babies 50 years ago, I hear gasps.

But in France, out of wedlock births stand at 6 in 10.

Not surprisingly, a recent survey by Pew Research of 34 European countries shows France to be one of the least religious.

Eleven percent in France say religion is very important in the their lives; 22 percent say they attend religious services at least monthly; 11 percent say they pray daily; and 11 percent say they believe in God with absolute certainty.

This is in stark contrast to the United States, where 49 percent say religion is very important to them; 36 percent say they attend religious services at least weekly; 55 percent say they pray daily; and 75 percent say they believe in God.

Only 47 percent of French people say marriage infidelity is morally unacceptable compared with 84 percent of Americans.

So although the hold of Christianity on the American public has weakened over the years, compared with France it remains a quite strong force.

This has important bearing on the welfare state crisis, at home and abroad.

As religion weakens, family structure weakens, and as family structure weakens, government strengthens and grows. Where people once looked to their parents to transmit values, love and care, increasingly they are looking to government.

The problem is that it doesn't work.

Traditional family and marriage reflect eternal values that cannot be replaced by government. These values — where husband and wife join in holy matrimony, embodying and transmitting truth that is greater than their own personal, egotistical proclivities — translate to children, learning, work, creativity and productivity.

In 1958, 82 percent of Americans said religion can solve "most or all of today's problems" and 7 percent said religion is "old-fashioned and out of date." By 2015, 57 percent said religion can solve our problems and 30 percent said religious is "out of date."

Over this period of time, American family structure significantly deteriorated and our welfare state, although still nowhere near what's happening in France, has become huge, bloated, and a major fiscal drain on the nation.

We surely should work to streamline and reform the welfare state.

But we shouldn't lose perspective that the core problem is the integrity of the traditional family. This is where our answers lie.

Trump's Important New Africa Strategy

December 19, 2018

President Donald Trump continues to take bold steps, recapturing America's exceptionalism at home and leadership abroad.

These important developments are too often getting drowned out by relentless noise in Washington, where the media obsess over many issues concerning this president except those most relevant to his job — his performance leading the nation to excellence.

A good example is the superlative new initiative just announced by National Security Advisor John Bolton establishing a new Africa strategy.

The initiative echoes the foreign policy vision Donald Trump articulated in his inaugural address.

That is, that America's relationship with the nations of the world should be defined first by our national interests. "We do not seek to impose our way of life on anyone," he said, "but rather to let it shine as an example for everyone to follow."

The Africa initiative is driven by three components: expanding and building new trade and commercial ties; containing radical Islamic terrorism and violent conflict; and assuring that American aid dollars are used effectively.

Among the concerns of the administration are aggressive moves by Russia and China into Africa, whose approach is far different than ours.

Corrupt regimes are an enormous problem in Africa. Both Russia and China see corruption as an opportunity for commercial gain by buying off regimes and building debt dependence through loans.

For instance, China, according to Bolton, is moving to take over the national power and utility company of Zambia to cover billions of dollars of debt.

The best-known public measure of corruption is the Corruption Perceptions Index published annually by Transparency International.

Countries are graded 1 to 100, 100 being corruption free — which, unfortunately, is nonexistent. The average global score is 43. The U.S. score is 75. The average score in Africa is 32.

China's scores is 41 and Russia is 29. It's clear that neither is motivated to further African development by cleaning up corruption. Quite the opposite.

However, disinfectant is not just the morally right thing to interject into African politics; it's also the economically right thing to do.

Plenty of research and experience point to the single most powerful potion for economic development and prosperity — economic freedom.

Economic freedom means limiting the size and scope of government, maintaining a reliable system of law and courts that protect property and contracts, keeping regulation to a necessary minimum, allowing citizens to trade freely abroad and keeping the nation's currency stable.

Average per capita income in nations that rank in the top 25 percent of economic freedom is $40,376. Average income in the bottom 25 percent is $5,649.

According to the World Bank, average per capita income in the 48 countries in sub-Saharan Africa was $1,464 in 2016.

It's no accident that African nations that are the most economically free also have the highest per capita incomes, such as Botswana, $7,596, and Seychelles, $15,505. These also are among the least corrupt countries in Africa according to Transparency International scores. It stands to reason that corruption is minimized when citizens have more freedom to do their own business and politicians have less power to interfere.

However, most African nations woefully lack economic freedom, which is why there is so much corruption and incomes are so low.

The Trump administration is right on target in advancing both American and African interests by moving "nations toward self-reliance and away from long-term dependency."

As is generally the case with welfare, foreign aid is notoriously ineffective and counterproductive, undermining self-reliance and fostering dependency.

U.S. aid to Africa in 2017 was $8.7 billion.

The new Africa strategy, by bringing to bear American ideals, will efficiently use our taxpayer funds and bring forth the great, unrealized potential of the African continent.

Protect Our Nation. Build the Wall

December 26, 2018

Somehow a Grinch always manages to show up to ruffle our Christmas spirit.

This year, the Grinch is the form of the Democratic leadership that is blocking the Christmas present that President Donald Trump wants to deliver to the nation in the form a wall to defend our southwestern border.

Trump wants $5 billion for the wall as part of a bill to continue funding the federal government. The Democrats say, "No," so now we're in another of the all too familiar standoffs, producing a government shutdown.

Why is this wall, which was a key component of the platform on which Trump ran and was elected, so important?

I spend a lot of time on airplanes. It has always struck me that when the flight crew delivers the message before takeoff about the possibility of using an oxygen mask, they note that adults traveling with children should don their mask, before helping the child.

It's counter to the instincts of most adults to do this. Which is why the instructions are explicitly given. You can't help your child, your neighbor or anybody else if you are not around to perform the task.

The first job is look after your own personal safety. This is true of nations as well as individuals.

Is building this wall on our southwestern border contrary to the message of the Statue of Liberty, which stands in New York harbor, inviting to our shores the world's "tired... poor... huddled masses, yearning to be free"?

Certainly not. The wall is about protecting our nation and making sure that it continues, strong and free, so that the distressed of the world can continue to see America as a light, a refuge and a bastion of the world's greatest ideals.

It just so happens that there are those around the world who are not huddled masses, but terrorists, drug dealers and others who want to undermine our national safety and integrity.

Let us recall that those who piloted the planes on that horrible day, Sept.11, 2001, leading to the deaths of more than 3,000 Americans, trained in our country during the presidency of Bill Clinton.

Latin America is a hotbed of unstable, despotic regimes that produce the horrible conditions causing so many to want to leave. Despotism produces dangerous bedfellows, and pernicious regimes around the world see these despotic regimes in Latin America as an opportunity for adventurism in our back yard.

The Wall Street Journal's Americas columnist Mary O'Grady has been regularly documenting this.

Just last week, she wrote about Russia's penetration in Latin America, quoting head of U.S. Southern Command, Adm. Kurt W. Tidd, that "Russia's increased role in our hemisphere is particularly concerning... could eventually transition from a regional spoiler to a critical threat to the U.S. homeland."

O'Grady also has written about the penetration of Iran into Latin America. "Iran has targeted Latin America since the mid-1980s by establishing mosques and cultural centers to spread the revolution," she writes.

The point is there are real threats. Would anyone have opposed spending $50 billion or $100 billion if it could have stopped 9/11?

The federal budget is now more than $4 trillion. We are talking here about $5 billion, one-tenth of 1 percent.

For perspective, in 1958, 60 percent of our federal budget went to defense and 25 percent went to social spending. Now 70 percent goes to social spending and less than 20 percent to defense.

Some very confused people want to claim this wall is about racism. That conclusion is only possible if you think defending our nation and the core principles that make it free is racist.

The American formula for diversity is "E Pluribus Unum." Out of many, one. Defending this is what this wall is about.

Let's hope President Trump prevails over the Democratic Grinch and succeeds in delivering this important Christmas present to the American people.

About the Author

Star Parker is one of the names on the short list of national black conservative leaders. She is the founder and president of the Center for Urban Renewal and Education

(CURE), a Washington D.C.-based public policy institute that promotes market-based solutions to fight poverty. Star consulted on federal Welfare Reform in the mid-90s and then founded CURE to bring new ideas to policy discussions on how to transition America's poor from government dependency. In 1996, she was a featured speaker at the 1996 Republican National Convention.

Before involvement in social activism, she had seven years of first-hand experience in the grip of welfare dependency. After a Christian conversion, she changed her life. Now, Star regularly consults with both federal and state legislators on market-based strategies to fight poverty.

In 2017, Star joined the White House Opportunity Initiative task force to share ideas on how to best fix our nation's most distressed zip codes. In 2018, she was appointed to the U.S. Frederick Douglass Bicentennial Commission.

Star has a bachelor's degree in Marketing and International Business from Woodbury University and has received numerous awards and commendations for her work on public policy issues. In 2016, CPAC honored her with the "Ronald Reagan Foot Soldier of the Year." In 2017, Star was the recipient of the Groundswell Impact award, and in 2018, Bott Radio Network presented Star with its annual Queen Esther award.

To date, Star Parker has spoken on more than 225 college campuses, including Harvard,

Berkeley, Emory, Liberty, Franciscan, UCLA and UVA. She has authored several books; is a regular commentator on national television and radio networks including the BBC, EWTN, and FOX News; and Star is a nationally syndicated columnist with Creators, reaching 7 million readers weekly.

~ ~ ~ ~ ~

America Divided
is also available as an e-book
for Kindle, Amazon Fire, iPad, Nook and
Android e-readers. Visit
creatorspublishing.com to learn more.

○ ○ ○

CREATORS PUBLISHING

We publish books.
We find compelling storytellers and
help them craft their narrative,
distributing their novels and collections
worldwide.

○ ○ ○

Made in the USA
Middletown, DE
13 October 2020